Guided by Your Light

Judi Stetson Weaver

Avid Readers Publishing Group
Lakewood, California

The opinions expressed in this manuscript are those of the author and do not represent the thoughts or opinions of the publisher. The author warrants and represents that she has the legal right to publish or own all material in this book. If you find a discrepancy, contact the publisher at www.avidreaderspg.com.

Guided by Your Light

All Rights Reserved

Copyright © 2015 Judi Stetson Weaver

Judi-Stetson@hotmail.com

This book may not be transmitted, reproduced, or stored in part or in whole by any means without the express written consent of the publisher except for brief quotations in articles and reviews.

Avid Readers Publishing Group

http://www.avidreaderspg.com

ISBN-13: 978-1-61286-274-3

Printed in the United States

PREFACE:

This life we are given on Mother Earth is a bounty of learning opportunities. The experience she provides us on this journey offer unlimited growth lessons, as our souls evolve. I believe the more time we take to look inside and see beyond the physical, the grander this life becomes. Everyone faces joys, challenges, celebrations, sorrows and life-altering events that shape the direction. More importantly, these experiences, as random as they may appear, serve our ultimate purpose and destiny.

This book is my journey and I offer it to you with loving intent as you travel in this earth school. Please take your time to work with me as we savor the experiences Creator sets on the path before us. God, the Great Spirit was crystal clear in directing me into this creation and as there truly are no coincidences. Your mindful reading of this soul-work book is destined for your development as well. The chapters in the book were shaped from development workshops, so please take time to follow the steps to achieve the most that you can from our journey together.

ACKNOWLEDGEMENTs

Many hearts and hands have supported this project. A very special thank you is given to my three amazing sons Steven, Dustin and Kevin, who have been my dearest teachers. To my loving husband Derek, I am so grateful for your patience and words of encouragement throughout this adventure. To Joan Whittemore, Diane Spears and Susan Forbes, I thank you for your valuable contributions to this book, making it into the quality teaching tool you see before you today. A special acknowledgement is given to my mother Agnes, my sister Tonia, Elena, family and friends who love me for all that I am.

Thank you, dear Creator for loving me enough to share your precious words with the world.

Judi Stetson-Weaver

CONTENTS

- INTRODUCTION 5
  - Personal History 5
    - TOPIC PREPERATION 8
- THE PRACTICE OF SPIRITUALITY & HEALING ENERGY 10
  - Lesson 1: Listening To Life 10
  - Lesson 2: Energy Healing 17
  - Lesson 3: The Fruit of the Spirit & Chakras 29
- PERSONAL DEVELOPMENT THROUGH SELF EXPLORATION 44
  - Lesson 4: Carrying the Weight of the World on Your Hips 44
  - Lesson 5: The Spirit of Love 50
  - Lesson 6: A True Warrior in Today's World 56
- CONNECTING WITH MOTHER EARTH TO BUILD YOUR SPIRITUALITY 65
  - Lesson 7: Drumming 65
  - Lesson 8: A World of Water 68
  - Lesson 9: Tree of Life 76
  - Lesson 10: Dance with a Dragonfly 88
  - Lesson 11: New Beginnings of Spiritual Knowledge Through Nature 94
  - Lesson 12: Fall-o-wing the Whispering Wings 100
- ADDENDUM 109
  - Eagle Clouds 109
- COMING FULL CIRCLE PERSONAL ANALYSIS 113
  - Review and Reflection 113
  - The Practice of Spirituality & Healing Energy 114
  - Personal Development Through Self Exploration 116
  - Connecting with Mother Earth to Build Your Spirituality 118
  - Review and Reflection Exercise 121
- INSPIRATIONAL MESSAGES 122
- EPILOGUE 126
- REFERENCE / RESOURCES 126
- SUGGESTED READING LIST 126

INTRODUCTION

Personal History

I think it is important to get an understanding of the author before you get into the workbook. It helps each of us to identify our Oneness. We are born of two parents, some of us have siblings. We may grow to have spouses, children and friends. Ultimately, we are here on this earth plane to fulfill a contracted destiny with God that we may spend a lifetime seeking to find. Eternal peace within is the highest essence of love.

It was the summer of 1998. My father was diagnosed with colon cancer. He had one tumor the size of a grapefruit which had broken through the intestinal wall. Another small tumor was later found and several lymph nodes were affected. The doctors had given him three months to live.

I always have had a strong Faith background and was baptized at age thirteen at a Southern Baptist Church. I regularly attended the First Church of Christ in Connecticut. Through the Church, I had facilitated several Bible study groups and Women's Retreats held at Camp Wrightman. My life has been filled with many challenges and my faith has always carried me and my loved ones. I have spent my life listening and trying to follow God's command whether I understood it or not.

One night while sleeping in the fall of 1998, I awoke in my bed and sat straight upright. I was told by Infinite Spirit that I needed to go to Florida and perform a healing on my father. I have never had such a calling and my father was adamant that he was a staunch atheist. Therefore, I struggled and questioned this calling greatly. I spent much time in prayer and meditation to this request. I told God I had no idea how, and if he really wanted me to perform this healing than he had to tell me how. He kept leading me to specific scripture until a Healing Plan was completed. I notified my sisters and the entire family. We all traveled from around the United States to Florida for Thanksgiving. I spoke to my pastor the day before leaving and told him what God had asked of me and that I needed healing oil. He was concerned and called me in for council immediately. After discussions, he mentioned various scriptures that could be useful, numerous times as he quoted specific scriptures I responded, "I already have that". Startled he looked at me and asked, "Who told you to choose that?" I told him God did and, his response was "It is a good thing that we have the same boss." He then gave me a bottle of anointing oil from Jerusalem. The healing went very well, my father's belief in God changed that day and after surgery and many prayers, he lived another nine years.

Throughout the years I was called to perform various healings on family members or sometimes strangers. I really don't know the outcomes, as there is no need. It is God's work not mine.

My life transitioned and I moved to Florida in 2000. As part of my spiritual journey, I attended a Reiki Class. I was greatly torn as to whether or not healing was something that I should actively pursue. Should

I wait until I was called to a specific person? There were six people scheduled for the class; however, all canceled except my girlfriend and me. During the session, Reverend Lyn Austin-Daniels, the teacher looked at me and asked, "Who is Jeff?" He was my brother-in-law who had passed. I had been guided to perform memorial services for him a few months earlier. It had been revealed to me that it had to be a Native American Ceremony and at the service I learned that his Grandmother was full blooded Cherokee. Many wonderful spiritual events happened that day. A large stork stared into my eyes, screeched at me and I felt him looking into my soul. A large flock of seagulls and other birds gathered and circled all of us near the end of the service. At the conclusion, a crow flew down from the sky, behind me and landed on my back. I felt its talons piercing my shirt. A huge surge of power mixed with fear ran through me but it was very evident that God and Jeff were with us. I recounted the story to Reverend Daniels. She said Jeff was behind me and encouraged me to move forward with this healing communication gift. We spent the day learning and getting attuned. At the end of the day I offered the Reverend a natural healing from me. She was amazed and felt as if power surged through her body and eliminated her health issue. I later learned that she made a comment about me having a hundred times more energy than her. We know this is not my power but God's. That day in the Reiki attunement class a spirit guide came to me. It was Moses in a long white robe and pointed cap. He walks with me to this day.

I have many stories such as these throughout the years including a visit to Cassadaga, Florida. I had registered for a Reiki 2 Class and was on my way, when I received a call it was canceled. I had prayed diligently and knew I was going in search of a spiritual day. So I left on a journey opening my heart to direction. I headed several places and kept ending in circles, I felt a bit lost, knowing that I needed to go to Cassadaga. I walked around town and into the Healing Gazebo and looked at the Healer Lorraine Peterson. We looked at one another and both knew we recognized each other. I used to be the director at local senior centers and she used to attend. Her presence, the peace, comfort and feelings that surged through me in the gazebo that day was amazing. I knew I had been called to this place as the next step of my spiritual development work.

My spiritual educational classes began. I visited Cassadaga, which is a small spiritual camp on a regular basis and attended classes for about a year and then decided to start tracking this information. I wanted to start a log of what I was learning. Not really knowing if or when it would become relevant, I did want to keep records. I attended the Temple services, Lyceum classes, Afternoon Message, various workshops and spent a great deal of time with Lorraine. I completed her healing classes and would visit with her while she worked in the gazebo to passively send healings while she worked with clients.

During the spring of 2011, when I first visited the Daytona Book & Metaphysical Shop I knew it was special and would play a major role in my life. I just didn't know how at that time.

I was lead to Mannie Billings' class, "Developing your Personal Relationship with the Infinite". I spent some time on the crystal bed prior to class. The class went well but I didn't feel any major changes. The next morning I woke up to find my entire great room and dining room filled with maggots. There was no known source and they weren't anywhere near the kitchen or garbage. I clearly heard Spirit tell me to,

"Research your Native American animal totems". Maggots fell within the same category as flies meaning death of old and rebirth of new. I knew Creator was working, but still didn't have a clear vision of what or where I was being lead. I was strongly directed to visit Cassadaga again on a Friday to visit Lorraine at the gazebo; however, it was closed when I arrived. I sat and prayed a while, when a woman came up to me. She was looking for a healing. We talked awhile and I provided a healing that she requested. After further discussion it was discovered that she was from Daytona and asked me why I didn't teach at the new store that was just opened at the Metaphysical Store. It was one of those moments in life where you know you are receiving a Spirit driven message. I was fully engulfed with God's love that teaching is what was being prepared me for and now was the time.

So I am supposed to teach! What is the topic? As Maya Angelou says, "As you learn, you teach." The answer to my heart question, was answered a few days later. It was early one morning when I went for a long walk along the beach and Creator clearly gave me specific topics and content. The list of class titles was fairly long, twenty-one for starters. I was to write a book, and the classes would be the foundation for the chapters. Three people attended my first class and nine the second. I only knew one person, but listening to how they came to be in the classes was the same as my teaching had been. Each person was clearly lead by Great Spirit.

I have attended over a thousand hours of formal study from around the world and thousands more of independent study and teaching. I have learned from many beautiful and faithful teachers including John of God the world famous healer in Abediania, Brazil. Training is essential to understand how to tap into your energy sources and to clearly follow the light. I am a Certified Healer through the International Association of Metaphysics. Every path may be slightly different but we are all on the same journey. Many people and organizations get caught up in ego and energy power trips. Be certain to use your natural discernment instincts when seeking enlightenment and teachers. When I was in Brazil with John of God during my healings God washed though me to the core and gifted me with a crystal enlightenment. I was clearly told that I was now a Crystal Light Healer. My true goal is to continue to tap into Universal Knowledge and share it with each of you. Now please gather something to write with and utilize the space allotted within this workbook and let's begin your journey!

TOPIC PREPERATION

When entering into each session it is very important to be connected to the topic of discussion. You need to be mindfully present to receive the gift which is being offered. It is important to follow these steps before each session:

1. It is necessary to be physically comfortable, so find a quiet time and place to begin.

2. You may want to play some music in the background to set a relaxing tone. Personally, I like melodies that can help ground me, earthen tones, animals, water, flutes or drums.

3. Our lives are all busy, but this is your sacred time. Take a few minutes to write down any thoughts and concerns that are running through your mind that might distract you from being in the moment. Now fold the paper and place it in your God box.

God Box

If you don't have one then this is your first project. Find a container with a lid and create your God/Great Spirit/Angel Box. The box is personally made to hold thoughts, worries or concerns. Leave them for God to watch over while you enter into this spiritual adventure.

After the class you may go back to the box to retrieve your list or you may do as I do and burn it. I gift it to the Universe. It has a much better understanding and greater level of resources to address the issues. Your mind will always create new ones, but for now choose to release these burdens.

4. Start with a blessing, a prayer or an acknowledgement of a greater power. Ask Holy Spirit for this special time to be blessed. Pray for wisdom, guidance and the ability to listen and understand the lesson that is planned for you this day.

5. Breathe. It is important to slow your breathing down, relax, and concentrate on each breath. Feel the movement of air naturally flowing through your body as your lungs expand and contract. Each inhalation provides life and sustenance to your body.

6. At the end of each session you will be returning to self. Become grounded back into your bodies and realign within the present. This may take a few minutes and deep breathing will help with this process.

7. Stay aware! Look, listen, feel the messages that are being directed towards you. The further you move into this process the more sensitive and attuned you become to communications that are coming to you. We are always being spoken to, the issue is do we know how to hear what is being said?

For the Meditations within the book you may want to prerecord them so that you can listen and truly receive the full experience of the mediation. Meditations can be used multiple times and your experiences will be different based on where you are.

At the end of each section there is a reflective section to write down what you experienced. This is critical to complete throughout the workbook. This is where you will be provided or guided with essential information for your growth and personal development.

Please take your time with this book! Plan each chapter as its own, one at a time. You will gather information in stages. Take time to reflect upon what you just experienced before you move on. When you open yourself to new experiences all the information may not come at once, but you will get additional information as time passes.

Note: Reference to God is for practical purposes. There are seventy-three names for God in major religions, so insert the term for which you are most comfortable.

THE PRACTICE OF SPIRITUALITY & HEALING ENERGY

Lesson 1: Listening To Life

EXERCISE I: INTRODUCTION

- ❖ What is communication with God?
- ❖ How does God communicate with you?
- ❖ Have you ever wondered why you don't hear God?
- ❖ Communication with God– what did I learn in church as a youth and what do I see today?

I think that it is important when studying a subject to first explore it analytically and then reflect upon it metaphysically. So let's get back to basics and break down what listening is. There are many types of listening, which is a critical component of communication.

Let's explore communication more closely and tap into listening with your heart to get a clearer direction for your future.

Communication – is the exchange of thoughts, messages, or information, as by speech, signals, writing, or behavior according to the Webster dictionary.

Without listening how can the exchange of communication be complete? So let's review the many types of listening.

EXERCISE II: INFORMATION

Types of Listening:

(Noted by changingminds.org)

Discriminative listening. The most basic type of listening, whereby the difference between sounds is identified. If you cannot hear differences, then you cannot make sense of the meaning that is expressed by such differences.

Listening is a visual as well as auditory act as we communicate much through body language. We also need to be able to discriminate between muscle and skeletal movements that signify different meanings.

James Borg states that 93% of communication comes through body language.

Comprehensive listening. The next step beyond discriminating between different sounds and sights is to make sense of them. To comprehend the meaning requires first having a lexicon of words at our fingertips and also all rules of grammar and syntax by which we can understand what others are saying.

Evaluative listening. In evaluative listening, or critical listening, we make judgments about what the other person are saying. We seek to assess the truth of what is being said. We also judge what people say against our values, assessing them as good or bad, worthy or unworthy. This also can be known as critical, judgmental or interpretive listening.

Critical listening. The purpose of this type of listening is to discern or judge by forming opinions about what is being said. Judgment includes assessing strengths, significant information, agreement and approval.

Bias listening. This happens when the person hears only what he wants to hear. He misinterprets based on preconceived notions about the speaker from previous experiences. Misconceptions of what is said can be stereotyped and filters listening often misses the meaning of the words spoken.

Appreciative listening. In this type of listening, we seek certain information which appeals to our moods and emotions that meets our needs and goals. We use appreciative listening when we are listening to favorite music, poetry or maybe even the stirring words of a great leader.

Sympathetic listening. We demonstrate we care about the speaker. We pay close attention and express our sorrow for their ills and happiness at their joys.

Empathic listening. We listen beyond sympathy to seek a truer understanding of how others are feeling. This requires excellent discrimination and close attention to the nuances of emotional signals. When we are being truly empathetic, we actually feel what they are feeling.

Therapeutic listening. The listener has a purpose of not only empathizing with the speaker but also to use this deep connection to help the speaker understand, change or develop in some way.

Dialogic listening. By learning through conversation and interchanging information, we actively seek to learn more about the person and how they think.

Relationship listening. Sometimes the most important factor in listening is to develop or sustain a relationship. This is why lovers talk for hours and attend closely to what each other has to say when the same words from someone else would seem to be rather boring.

Extrasensory Perception

Now it is time to look at listening internally through perceptions. There are four primary types of human extrasensory perceptions. Many people use a combination of these. But it is not uncommon to have one more developed than the rest.

Perception. According to the Latin, perception (percipio) is the process of attaining awareness or understanding of the environment by organizing and interpreting sensory information.

It is believed that certain people are born with a heightened perception of Spirit (i.e. natural psychics), but the truth of the matter is, that we all have a spirit or soul, as well as a physical body. Therefore, we are all essentially spirit, so spirit communication is a natural and perfectly normal phenomenon.

There are four types of receiving psychic information. They are as follows:

Clairvoyance. The power to see objects or events that cannot be perceived by the senses. Acute intuitive insight or perceptiveness

Clairaudience. The power to hear things outside the range of normal perception

Clairsentience. Also known as psychometry, is the ability to hold an object or touch someone and receive information.

Knowing. Beyond intuition, this gift is demonstrated by possessing knowledge, information, or understanding.

Terms noted within the *Webster Dictionary*

As previously stated, anyone and everyone has the ability to tap into sensory perception. Do you see any of these being more prominent within yourself? When you are listening to someone, is there a little voice, a feeling in your gut, unexplained things, light flashes/balls or body feelings such as chills, hair rising, peace, comfort, trembling or a rush of energy on occasion?

We have taken some time considering types of listening and perception. Now it is time to look within. This is a guided meditation please read this slowly (or pre-record), and take time to reflect as you work your way through the meditation.

EXERCISE III: Meditation

Listening To Life

Find a quiet place to sit and relax. Be certain that all phones are shut off and you will be uninterrupted for about ten minutes. Sit quietly and start to slow down and take some deep cleansing breaths in and out. Sit comfortably in a chair with your feet flat on the ground. You may want to take off your shoes and leave your palms facing upward in your lap. With each breath try to relax more and more. Breathe in and out… in and out. Let your body become loose, feel the stress and tension float away. Try to quiet your mind, slow it down. Move through this meditation one word and moment at a time. Let your thoughts clear away, when one comes in gently release it with blessings to return if necessary at another time. Breathe deeply in and then out once more.

Envision a white light that is gently coming down to surround you – slowly filling you with peace, love and protection as we move forward. Ask your Higher Power God Source for the ability to hear the information and guidance that is being sent.

Sit comfortably and listen quietly to your surroundings, to the soothing music and now begin to listen to how you and your body may feel. Thoughts, information and ideas that you want to remember gently place in your memory bag to take out when this exercise is over.

Acknowledge your body and its voice. Release the stress and just listen to the sensations that you are experiencing at this moment.

Now let's open up your body one area at a time. Take a pause at each area. Concentrate and feel your bones, the joints and most especially your skin.

Be still and listen to your head, to your neck, your shoulders and gently work down each arm slowly to your wrists and then to your hands and each finger.

Follow your body down your spine from the neck all the way through each disc in your back one at a time and listen.

Continue down into and along each leg, your knees and then into your ankles, feet and each toe.

Be still in this presence.

Listen to your body:

    All the mentioned parts – your cells, muscles, joints, veins, capillaries, nerves, and bones.

    Listen to the moment.

    Listen to the air.

    Listen with your heart.

    Listen with your internal voice.

    Listen to the sun.

    Listen to your Higher Power.

Listen to your guides.

Be still and present. Stay in this space for several minutes. Stay in the total peace and silence of this space so that information and communication from beyond can easily penetrate your being.

Be still … feel … and listen.

It is time to slowly come back. Take a breath in and out, say thank you to your higher power/God source for this time, for their knowledge and for being. Take another deep breath in and out you are now returning to this room and time. Take your time coming back there is no hurry just a peaceful transition of space and time – slowly open your eyes when you feel ready.

EXERCISE IV: SELF REFLECTION

Take a few minutes to reflect upon what you have just experienced. Please write:

What did you see?
_____
_____
_____
_____

What did you feel?
_____
_____
_____
_____

What did you hear?
_____
_____
_____
_____

What did you experience?

_____
_____
_____
_____

Do not judge what you received, it is information. It may make sense to you now or it may be just a part of the puzzle. Please write it down for future reference.

_____
_____
_____
_____
_____

Did you notice an internal dialogue, a small voice, whispering thoughts, ideas to pursue, emotions, images of information? This process is not a onetime experience to be mastered in a few minutes, but takes time and practice. The more time and practice you put into it the easier it is to tap into the information that is being given to you.

The key to listening with your soul or heart is to be attentive to what is being relayed to you. Take note of nature. Do you see or feel a particular way when you see a being or when you are at a specific location? What is the information being relayed in the moment? Life is an ongoing lesson. Are you aware of the chapters that are being written around you? Take time to listen to words, expressions, perceptions and spiritual guidance.

_____
_____
_____
_____

Once that information is received, accept it as truth. Do not always listen to others and value their opinions and/or information over your own. The communications that you receive are specific and true to you and your existence. This is a gift, be sure to honor that truth for what it is: a lesson for you and you alone.

God, and your guides have been working your entire lifetime to get your attention and are eagerly waiting for you to walk through the next door. Be well and listen – truly listen with your ears, heart, soul and entire essence to what is being communicated.

Notes to self:
_____
_____
_____
_____
_____

EXERCISE V: HOMEWORK

Plan a few minutes every day to be present in the moment. You can easily plan this for anywhere in your life. On a lunch break or coffee break. Maybe in car waiting to pick up the kids. It doesn't matter where you are just take a minute or two and listen. Quiet your mind, be still and listen. Just breathe deeply a few times, stop and listen beyond your ears and hear with your soul.

_____
_____
_____
_____
_____
_____

For best results plan for one lesson at each session.

Lesson 2: Energy Healing

EXERCISE I: INTRODUCTION

Join me in exploring the gift of healing energies and how it works through you. We will discuss: grounding, cleansing, protection, channeling, listening to God and the various techniques used in energy healings. First I would like to explain some concepts that you may not be familiar with. Energy healing is a term that is mostly heard in holistic therapies where energy enters the body and works to realign and balance the body to its highest functioning natural structure. The energy itself is the light or love of God which is passed into your body through focus and intention to receive. The energy enters the body through your crown chakra.

Each human body has nine vital energy centers that are aligned in front of your spine. Seven are inside of your body and two above your head. There is the crown chakra which is located on the top of your head; the third eye which is in the center of your forehead; the throat chakra is in front of throat; the heart chakra is located in the center of your chest; the solar plexus chakra is located below the ribs; the sacral chakra is located just below the belly button and the root chakra is located near the base of the spine. Each of these energy centers are highly active in the overall functioning of your body. We will discuss this in greater detail further along in the book.

Let's move forward and learn about spiritual healing and how you can tap into your gifts and talents. The most important lessons to remember is that the energy being used is God's and you are allowing this energy to enter into your body for the healing. God has amazing healing energy that is available to each of us for whatever the need. It is, however, up to each of us to be faithful and trusting enough to allow God to use our bodies as a vessel through which the energy flows.

Envision a straw is running through the center of your being. It starts at the top of your head runs all the way through you to the floor. There is an additional exit through your hands. Being grounded is a crucial step of the process as you allow the energy to flow into your crown chakra and out your hands. Energy healings can be performed on yourself or passed through you to another.

EXERCISE II: INFORMATION

Grounding

Grounding is to see yourself fully rooted to an area before you begin to work with a person. Ask for a prayer of protection before you begin and to be grounded through the healing and energy work. The following is an example from the Cassadaga Church and is by no means the only type of prayer that may be used:

Father – Mother God, I ask that I be cleared and cleansed within the universal White Christ light, the green healing light and the purple transmuting flame. Within God's will and for my highest good I ask that any and all negativity and/or evil be completely sealed in its own light, encapsulated within the ultra-

violet light, cut off and removed from me. Impersonally, with neither love nor hate, I return all negativity and/or evil to its source of emanation, decreeing that it never again be allowed to re-establish itself within me or anyone else in any form. I now ask that I be placed within a triple capsule of the universal White Christ light of protection, and for this blessing, I give thanks.

Father God I pray that you work with me at this time as I enter into this healing ceremony. Allow me to be a pure vessel, so that your love and light can easily pass through my body for the highest and best of all involved. I pray that you God, all Angels, Spirit Guides, Healing entities, and loved ones of the highest intention come forth for this healing. I pray for protection and grounding of my personal body and that only loving light will be used in this healing.

A Healing can be physical, spiritual, emotional or mental. It is not your place to say what should be or needs to be healed. God knows what the healing is to be!

So let's take time to review a bit of research. Energy is Universal and it has been proven that energy just doesn't dissipate. It can change forms but never truly disappears. Einstein states that $E=MC^2$. What does happen to energy?

"In 1877, Peter Guthrie Tait claimed that the principle originated with Sir Isaac Newton, based on a creative reading of propositions 40 and 41 of the Philosophiae Naturalis Principia Mathematica. This article is about the physics principle. For information on using energy resources sustainably, see Energy conservation.

Conservation of energy states that the total amount of energy in an isolated system remains constant, although it may change forms (for instance, friction turns kinetic energy into thermal energy). In thermodynamics, the first law of thermodynamics is a statement of the conservation of energy for thermodynamic systems.

Put simply, the law of conservation of energy states that energy cannot be created (made from nothing), or destroyed (made to disappear to no-where) and that energy can be changed from one form to another (such as electrical energy into heat energy).

The energy conservation law is a mathematical consequence of the shift symmetry of time; energy conservation is implied by the empirical fact that physical laws remain the same over time."

Another example would be water. It can't be made and never disappears. It just changes form. It can fall as rain, evaporate with the sun, build within the clouds and fall again as rain, be frozen and fall as snow or hail. Water is water whether it is as a liquid, vapor or solid.

The same could be said of the Trinity the Father God, the Son and the Holy Ghost all are of one. It is the same principle in the spiritual laws of energy.

What is Energy Healing?

Energy healing shows itself in the physical, emotional, mental and spiritual change in the individual. These changes can be noticeable to everybody or they can be subtle and only felt by the person channeling or receiving the healing. It could be a change from physical sickness to recovery. Finding peace or emotional calmness is another aspect of change that is seen as a person goes through the process of spiritual healing.

The most dramatic and exciting part of the process is when one is able to have a clearer vision of God and how we relate to God and each other. This unity of guidance and love redefines a person's life and their direction in terms of career, interpersonal relationships and spiritual growth.

God knows each of His children and loves them for exactly who and what they are. He also wants the highest and best for each of his children. God also will very carefully and skillfully align time, space and beings into perfect unification so that a vibrational healing is possible. The trained and willing healer is available and the recipient is open to receive God's energy and channel it down to a person who is open to receive this holy vibration.

A healer is a facilitator of this process. A spiritual healer has the ability to "see" the persons etheric body as a whole greater than the sum of their parts. The healers' job is to help remove blocks to an individual's growth.

How a spiritual healer does his/her job varies from person to person. There are a number of types of healers working through different modalities all using the same God Force or Source for their healings techniques. Examples are: Reiki, Healing Touch, Pranic Healing, Shamanism, Therapeutic Touch, Emotional Freedom Techniques (EFT), Reflexology, Quantum Touch and Esoteric Healing to name a few.

Most accomplished healers have the ability to see the blocks or the blockages that are causing the problems in the lives of their clients. The blockage can be physical, emotional, mental or spiritual. Through a combination of talking to the client, information gathered through spirt by the healer, the energy healing itself, the client is brought from their current state to a place of balance.

A spiritual healer may only see a person once or twice or a person may return often. A person may also request and receive a healing from a distanced location-that is known as intercessory healing. They could be communicating through a phone line or it could just be sent and received. Remember, energy just changes form!

Common Elements of Healing Techniques

Many different cultures throughout history have used healing arts that use touch to transfer healing energy. Early references to this appear in both Eastern and Western writings. In the *History of the Jin Dynasty*, it says: "Those who cultivate the Dao and nourish the qi are able… to spread qi to others." (Cohen, 245), Hippocrates referred to the bio field as "the force which flows from many people's hands." Quoted in NIH report. Energy healing is often passed down by oral tradition, and is found in many places around the world including: China, Japan, and other Asian countries, India, Peru, Australia, Polynesian Islands, and amongst Native American tribes. An exploration of these traditions and several modern techniques for energy healing reveals several common elements, which are described below.

Who Can Heal?

Energy healing is an innate human skill. Even young children are quite effective at it because their minds don't block the channel. Training in healing techniques, study of energy theory, and knowledge of physical anatomy help to refine the work and boost its power, but they're not essential. Anyone can be a healer as long as you are open to channel the energy flow to another.

Before practicing healing on others, the practitioner should do the necessary work to bring their own system into balance and clear his/her own blockages. After that, he/she will be better able to provide healing energy to the client. Therefore it is important for a practitioner to learn some basic techniques to do so. The practitioner will begin by grounding themselves, provide an energy self-check where they visualize that all chakras circulating and the appropriate energy colors are aligned. The healer must feel relaxed and also be physically feeling well. If a healer happens to have a cold it isn't a good time to practice their ability.

The role of the client is to be open and willing to change. The natural tendency of blocked energy is to move towards release, and the natural tendency of the body is to move toward balance. If the client can be receptive to healing, the healer simply nudges the client's energy, and the client's soul will guide the healing.

Why Do We Need Healing?

Our energy pathways should be free-flowing, actively circulating to clear stagnant energies and bring in fresh, healthy energy. However, the pathways can become blocked, and healing may be helpful in removing those blockages.

A blockage can occur in any areas of our bodies and an example might be emotional pain, physical illness, depravation of needs, unfulfilled or disappointment of self. Negative energy that has slowed or stagnated the free flow of energy. There is a direct relationship between emotional trauma and physical dis-ease.

What is the mechanism for healing? There are several theories, which can be condensed to a few major concepts.

Cleansing. The Practitioner helps to clear blockages, and encourages stagnant energy into motion. The body is in constant motion including down to its molecular structure. Keeping this free flow of energy keeps the body performing at its optimum. Oftentimes a physical cleansing is performed by burning sage as traditionally practiced by Native Americans.

Resonance (Re-structuring). The Practitioner holds the highest vibration possible, creating a model of balanced energy, gently guiding the client's energy vibration, which will naturally entrain itself to match the practitioner's balanced system. The practitioner's energy is giving instructions to the client's energy, and providing a structure for them to organize their scattered energies.

Channeling (Jump-starting). The Practitioner accesses Universal energy, and helps to guide it into the client's system. The client's energy system has an innate wisdom, which will then guide the healing energies to where they are most needed. The practitioner is functioning as jumper cables, stimulating the energy flow in the client's body, the increased energy helps to clear blockages.

How Does Healing Work?

Healing is done through interaction of the practitioner's with the client's energy field. Some techniques believe this is best accomplished by the practitioner laying his hands directly on the client's body and working with very light touch. Some techniques instruct the healer to work with his hands a few inches above client's body so his/her energy field is interacting with client's energy field directly.

Intent is key. The practitioner works with Intention, a conscious desire to aid the client in healing. In turn, the client must agree to receive the energy, so that the healing may occur. Some believe that the key intention of energy exchange is through a person's eyes, which are known as the "windows of the soul".

Energy centers and pathways. It is helpful to have a knowledge of theories about energy centers (i.e. chakras), energy flows (i.e. meridians), and points where the energy is most accessible (i.e. acupuncture points). By working with these structures when placing her hands in healing positions, the practitioner is able to more accurately target her energy.

Multi-dimensional. Energy healing works on several levels at once: spiritual, emotional, mental, and physical. It's most beneficial applications involve awareness of this aspect, and intentionally use it for healing one or more types of issues.

Emotional Release. Often something that manifests as physical illness is rooted in deeper emotional or spiritual issues. During energy work, a client may have an emotional release that might be accompanied by specific memories, or may be experienced as pure emotion, which arises "for no reason." Releases may be dramatic, with tears, or other expressions of trauma memory. If the practitioner and client stay centered and continue energy work, the emotion can be fully released from the blockage within the energy field.

Spiritual Growth. Energy medicine is an inherently spiritual practice and can lead to spiritual growth for both practitioner and client. It can create a change in consciousness, which allows us to feel a deeper sense of connection to the energies of other people, and the natural world around us.

Effects of Healing

Techniques vary widely, and the types of illness of which are addressed varies widely; however, there are several common outcomes to all forms of energy healing:

- Acceleration of wound healing
- Reduction of the pain of thermal burns
- Acceleration of healing time
- Reduction of sunburn pain and coloration
- Reduction of acute and chronic pain
- Reduction of anxiety
- Release of pent-up grief *(NIH report)*

Most techniques produce a deep relaxation within a short period of time, and thus can be excellent for people experiencing stress related dis-ease. Resting after a session allows the body to recover. Also it is important to drink a lot of water to assist in flushing body toxins from the system.

Diseases may develop over a long period of time or they may have a sudden onset such as an accident. Sometimes healing is a slow process, where the practitioner starts a process in motion. The client continues to improve his/her condition through diet, lifestyle changes, exercise, counseling, medical treatments, and more energy work. Other times, healing may be a quantum leap, with significant, long-lasting changes taking place after minutes of healing. Generally, the more chronic the concern, the more energy work is needed to release long-held patterns.

Generally, the larger the trauma or the more severe the illness, the quicker and more dramatic the results. When someone is only slightly out of balance, the effects of healing may not be obvious. When someone's energy is radically out of balance, a shift toward health may be more immediately evident.

Healing is an on-going process, not an end result. Having energy healing done once doesn't mean you'll never be ill again. There are continual challenges to our energy systems. Having a routine practice of energy work such as qi gong helps with keeping a balanced energy system. Healing emotional traumas and physical energies as soon as possible is helpful because it prevents injuries from becoming deeply entrenched in the energetic or etheric system.

The practitioner accesses unlimited Universal Energy during healing, and thus should feel energized at the end of a healing session. If the practitioner feels drained at the end of the session, it indicates that he/she was attempting to use personal, energy to heal, instead of being in the Universal Flow.

Hands-on energy healing is a versatile, diverse healing modality. It can be combined with other hands-on healing techniques with excellent results. Also is a useful complementary therapy to traditional medicine and psychotherapy. It can be supplemented with other techniques such as sound therapy, or color therapy to boost its effectiveness. It is useful for a wide variety of physical, mental, and emotional illnesses and imbalances. Techniques can also be used on plants and animals, as well as in distance healing.

It is possible to charge inanimate objects with Universal Energy, and then use them for healing. For example, charging a glass of water for a client to drink enhances a treatment. Another example would be to charge minerals or religious artifacts.

Contraindications/Potential Concerns

There are several theories which claim that energy medicine can only have positive effects, and can do no harm. They say that if the practitioner sends "too much" energy, the client's body will just let it pass on through, and if hands are placed "wrongly" the client's energy pathways will simply carry the energy to where it is needed. In a workshop on Intuitive Energy Medicine, Suzanne Louise demonstrated that if you purposely run a meridian in reverse, it causes the client to feel jittery and uncomfortable, but if you "accidentally" run it backwards but with full healing intent, the touch functions in a healing manner.

Some theories particularly those which emphasize polarity directions of the energy flow, purport that it is possible to give the client too much energy, or to run the energy in the wrong direction. Signs of an energy overdose or misalignment is as follows: increasing restlessness, irritability, anxiety, hostility, pain, dizziness, nausea.

Although there are many books available which teach the theory and practice of energy healing, it is important practitioners also attend healing workshops, or work with a reputable teacher. This will give them a better grasp of the nuances of the techniques, and also give them someone to double-check their observations, and supervise their initial work. My personal protocol follows.

<u>Healing Practice</u>

First ask, "Would you like a healing?" Once permission is granted I talk to the person to see if they understand what healing is. I briefly tell them that I was called to perform healings years ago and have been practicing as God has directed me since that time. I explain this is not my energy but I am just a vessel for Him to use. It is God's energy that passes through me. I explain the process, the importance of them believing and placing their intention towards what they want healed. They don't have to say a word and I don't need to know anything including their name. I discuss the heat of the energy and colors they may feel or see and are instructed just to relax and enjoy. I also ask if I may place my hands on their shoulders and back if directed. I explain the continuation of healing energy for 72 hours and the importance of not discussing the healing during this time period.

I stand behind the person and begin in prayer first thanking God and Jesus for this opportunity and then asking them for a prayer of protection during this time for myself. I envision a large white light flowing through a tube that runs from the top of my head through my body. I pray to stay out of God's way as God performs this healing. I continue to ask for God to come forth, Jesus to come forth, my healing guides, Moses, Arch Angel Raphael, any and all healing guides and loving healing sprits who want to come forth for the healing of this child of God. I keep my eyes closed and hold my hands in a position of prayer. After feeling the vibration build I place my hands above their head and begin. Throughout the healing I continue to pray for healing, peace, love, health for this child of God and listen for direction. I get either a thought, a body pain or sometimes I can mentally visualize into a body part that needs the focused healing energy. I work on an area until I feel directed to a new area or I feel the power bouncing from one palm to the other being consistent. I generally always hold a hand on each side of the body, following the chakra's and let the energy pass through for an even and balanced healing. Sometimes I know what the issues are and other times I do not. It doesn't matter because I know God does and He knows what is being healed. I may see and feel colors, or other spirit guides that may come forth. A true affirmation for me is when I am called to a specific area of the body and the energy flow is greatly increased and my breathing pattern deepens – I know I am at an area of need area until the energy and breathing slows again. Sometimes I know when things are blocked, need removal or to be destroyed by God's energy. I may see the illness as color that bursts. I often envision healthy blood and call forth new healthy cells for rebuilding, to provide strength and good health to all of the body parts.

I estimate the healing process to be about 6-8 minutes in length and throughout that time I remain in prayer. Sometimes I am drawn back to a same area for a second time at the closing of the process for just a bit more energy. I will move back to the crown chakra as the energy is completing and I begin to close. I spend that time praising God, Jesus and all the entities who came forth for this loving child of God, thanking them for their love and blessings around this healing. I then bring my hands back to a prayer position and end the prayer of thanksgiving. I lean forward and end with a small statement such as "May God's love and peace be with you and your healing".

Prepare the Receiver

1. Have the person sit comfortably in a chair facing East with their feet touching the ground and palms relaxed on their lap facing open towards the sky.

2. Give a brief description of what you are going to do.

3. Explain examples of what they may experience – colors, heat, visions, physical sensations.

4. Ask the receiver to believe the healing is taking place. Think about what they are seeking healing for and to have intention in mind if they would like to. If nothing specific comes to mind then just be open to the healing.

5. The healing will continue for up to 72 hours.

6. Drink plenty of fluids during this period of time.

7. Do not discuss the healing with others until after the healing is complete. Others may be well intentioned but their opinions and negative energies can easily affect the healing.

Prepare Yourself

1. Quiet yourself.

2. Get grounded.

3. Open yourself in prayer.

4. Call for a prayer of protection.

5. Call in God, angels, healers, Arch Angel Raphael (healing angel), guides, any and all loved ones to assist in healing this loving child of God.

6. Healing energy is often known as "White Light," which is God's purest love.

Healing Process

Allow the energy or white light to flow through your body. Remember, you are just a channel for this use.

1. Continue to pray for this person during the healing for good health, happiness and love.

2. You may experience thoughts, body aches, pulsing sensations, heat, colors or knowledge as to areas that you need to concentrate your hands towards. The sensation will change and then you will know when to move to the next area. You do not need to touch the body directly. You may choose to touch the client, as it comforts some but if so, remember to ask the person first and be mindful to never touch inappropriate areas.

3. When you feel that the energy is slowing down or closing, you can end the healing. Say a prayer of gratitude for the healing that has taken place and end in love for your higher power for this child of God and the blessing of healing.

4. Quietly say a verbal blessing to the recipient such as, "May God's love and peace be with you and your healing". This also will let the person know the healing has ended.

After Thoughts

1. Whether or not there should be any discussion after the healing between the healer and the client is undetermined.

2. The healer must always maintain the best and highest intention of the healing to the client.

3. The healer may know the ailments of the client; however, the healer doesn't know if God just healed the physical aspect of the illness. Keep your knowledge, and influence out of the intervention.

4. My personal style is to affirm with the client what they choose to share about the experience. By following their lead, God provides information that I need to share, again only with the highest intention of goodness. The healing will continue for a minimum of 72 hours and it is important that the client drink plenty of water during this time as the body is flushing out impurities.

Side Bar. It has been found that there is a definite weight that is directly correlated to a human soul. There have been various studies to justify this statement. Below is one such example.

In 1907, MacDougall weighed six patients while they were in the process of dying from tuberculosis in an old age home. It was relatively easy to determine when death was only a few hours away, and at this point the entire bed was placed on an industrial sized scale which was sensitive to the gram. He took his results (a varying amount of perceived mass loss in most of the six cases) to support his hypothesis that the soul had mass, and when the soul departed the body, so did this mass. The determination of the soul weighing 21 grams was based on the average loss of mass in the six patients within minutes or hours after death. Experiments on mice and other animals took place. Most notably the weighing upon death of sheep seemed to create mass for a few minutes which later disappeared. The hypothesis was made that a soul portal formed upon death which then whisked the soul away.

In conclusion, each healing session is unique and can be a different experience. It is a beautiful gift to be a participant in a healing process. As a person continues to practice healings more often the connection to spirit is strengthened and the communication level increases. I believe the healing takes place no matter how much experience you have it is all a matter of being clear and open to allow the pure flow of God's love to radiate into the person who is requesting the healing. It is a true blessing to be a part of this process!

As you are working within this study guide, it is important to experience as much of this process first hand to begin to understand what is happening both within you and what is happening in the world around you. Please follow the guidelines that I have provided and experiment yourself. You have the ability within you, just tap into it and you are able to practice within your own body. Don't stop because you feel stupid and believe that someone is watching you. They aren't. This is your time to tap into energy much greater than yourself to benefit your body, mind and spirit. Please don't rush yourself. Just relax, take the time, tap into the white light and begin.

EXERCISE III: MEDITATION

Self-Healing Meditation

Find a quiet place to sit and relax. Be certain that all phones are shut off and you will be uninterrupted for about ten minutes. Sit quietly. Close your eyes and take five deep breaths in and out slowly and deeply. Sit in a comfortable position with your feet on the ground and your palms up in your lap. With each breath feel your body relaxing more and more. In and out. In and out. Let the thoughts and worries float away and just enjoy the peaceful bliss of this time.

Now that you are fully relaxed pray to your higher spirit, God, Great Spirit, Jesus, Angels and all Spirit Guides. Ask all to come to you at this time to perform this healing. Ask for them to enter within. Envision the white light which is God's pure love flowing into the top of your head your crown chakra. Allow this light to flow into your body. Allow the love to slowly enter each area mentioned and move throughout your body as a single fluid entity. Bring the energy into your head, and forehead which is also your third eye, allow it to flow into your face, ears, around your brain and travel lower into your neck. Envision this pure white light gently flowing and filling within and around all parts of your body, arms, shoulders, elbows, wrists, fingers, hands, your chest, welcome the light into all organs of your body. Your heart, lungs, liver, intestines, your veins, muscle tissue, bones, circulation systems, neurological systems, thyroid, reproductive systems and hormonal functions. Encourage the energy to gather and move down through your central core. Let the energy continue to flow down through your legs, thighs, knees, ankles, feet and toes. The energy and pulsing continues to flow within and move through all areas of your entire existence. Stay in this space and pause. Feel God's love and light pulse within all areas of your body. It is time to change direction and to moving upward once again. This time you will be traveling up the backside of your body. Travel upward focusing on your legs, bottom, hips and then your spine. Move slowly and allow the energy to flow through each and every vertebra of the spine. The energy moves in perfect alignment and synchronicity through your entire body pulsing one with God. You are but the same, His loving healing light that is permeating throughout your body in the same rhythm of your heart beat. Stay in this place and pause. Just feel the light as it reverberates throughout your body. Moving back and forth, circling, pulsing, and flowing throughout. If there is an area that you want to focus on stay in that space of absorption a bit longer. Feel the energy, see the light, colors, feel the warmth. Know the complete and total acceptance of the perfect being that you are is loved beyond and within all that is.

The pulses are becoming softer now and therefore it is time to close this session. Feel the light move back up to your crown chakra and allow it to close once again. You will still feel the higher vibration of light and healing within your body as the healing continues to work. Thank God, the Angels, Healers, Spirit Guides and past loved ones for coming to you this day.

EXERCISE IV: SELF REFLECTION

Now that the healing has ended remember that it will continue to last for the next 72 hours. Be sure to increase your intake of water and don't discuss the healing and what transpired until after the healing has totally ended. Now it is time to reflect on your experience. This is the most important step of the process.

What did you see?

_____
_____
_____
_____
_____

What did you feel?

_____
_____
_____
_____
_____

What did you hear?

_____
_____
_____
_____
_____

What did you experience?

_____
_____
_____
_____
_____

Notes to self:

_____
_____
_____
_____
_____

EXERCISE V: Homework

Healing with energy and the moving of energy takes practice. Plan to sit and quiet yourself and then open yourself to allowing the energy to move yourself. You may want to practice this by sending loving energy to your pet if you have one. You may also send this same loving energy to animals that are outside. It is fascinating to sometimes see and experience their reaction to the positive and healing energy that flows to them.

_____
_____
_____
_____
_____

For best results plan for one lesson at each session.

Lesson 3: The Fruit of the Spirit & Chakras

EXERCISE I: INTRODUCTION

There are so many various levels of energy that are intertwined with faith and how we understand it. We will discuss Chakras, auras, colors, the fruits of the spirits within the Bible, animals, minerals, etheric levels, various planes along with their hierarchy and the Lord's Prayer.

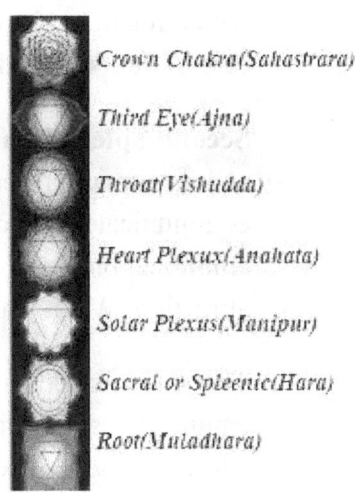

Crown Chakra (Sahastrara)
Third Eye (Ajna)
Throat (Vishudda)
Heart Plexux (Anahata)
Solar Plexus (Manipur)
Sacral or Spleenic (Hara)
Root (Muladhara)

This chapter may seem very complicated to understand. Please be patient with yourself as we explore each area independently. There are energy centers within each of our bodies that correlate to various specific areas. It is essential when learning about healing work to get an understanding of these energy centers and how they operate.

EXERCISE II: INFORMATION

What are Chakras?

Chakras: There are seven vital energy centers where spiritual energy flows inside the body. They are located in line with the spine. Each energy center contains information relating to different aspects of your being. See above a diagram of the unique functions and blockages of the seven centers.

Chakra Healing: By increasing energy focus blocks in particular areas of the body are released, creating more flow through these energy centers. There is a direct correspondence of these vital energy sources in the hands, feet and ear. Discover the most effective tools for balancing and healing the chakras.

Chakra Colors. The colors can change in these energy centers at the same time. Your mood, what you're experiencing, and other people energies, all determine the colors of a chakras.

Chakra Meditation. Meditating develops awareness of energy, supports releasing personal blocks, and helps you create a healthy flow in your system. Practice centering and grounding. Give yourself a healing with this chakra meditation.

The Seven Chakras

First Root Chakra. Located near the base of the spine, the first chakra is the energy and information center relating to survival as spirit in body. As a spiritual being, you have your own unique survival information. Along your journey, what you need to do to survive will be different than what others need to do. The first chakra is the energy center for issues relating to work, livelihood and money.

The root chakra includes information about belonging to a group, fear and security issues. Issues which relate to blocks in the first chakra include may include problems with finances, not taking care of yourself, and unfounded fears.

Second Spleen Chakra. Located a few finger widths below navel, the second chakra is the energy and information center relating to emotionality, sexuality and clairsentience. As spirit, you communicate with your body through a wide range of emotions. Many issues are rooted in emotional blockages in the second chakra. The second chakra is the information center for sexual attraction. When you are attracted to someone, your second chakra will spin faster and tingle!

The spleen chakra is the energy center for clairsentience, which is your ability to sense others' emotions. Issues which relate to blocks in the second chakra include not feeling your true emotions, a lack of healthy sexual boundaries and mistaking others' emotions for your own.

Third Solar Plexus Chakra. Located at the solar plexus, just below the ribs, the third chakra is the information center for energy distribution and personal power. Your third chakra distributes energy throughout your personal energy system. This chakra relates to how much energy you have, how you use it and what you use it for. Some use their energy to empower themselves. Some use their energy to manipulate others.

The solar plexus chakra is also the seat of the ego identity, who your mind thinks you are. Issues which relate to blocks in the third chakra include low or erratic energy levels, playing power games, and not being your authentic Self.

Fourth Heart Chakra. Located in the center of the chest area, the fourth chakra is the energy center for love, validation, and your ability to be at peace. The fourth chakra is the information center for what you love, what you're in affinity with, and to what you're magnetically drawn to. The fourth chakra relates to validation, your sense of self-worth, and self-love.

The heart chakra is about your ability to be at peace with people, places and objects. Issues relating to blocks in the fourth chakra may include losing touch with what you love, feeling unworthy, and not forgiving yourself or others.

Fifth Throat Chakra. Located at the base of the neck and throat, the fifth chakra is the information center for communication and self-expression communicating both to others and to yourself. It contains information about expressing yourself verbally and vocally, through song. The fifth chakra allows you to listen to and express your inner voice.

The throat chakra relates to psychic levels of communication as in clairaudience, telepathy, and channeling abilities. Issues relating to blocks in the fifth chakra may include poor communication, not listening to your inner voice, and confusion from hearing other voices.

Sixth Third Eye Chakra. Located through the center of the head, in line with the forehead in the center of the eyebrow ridge, the sixth chakra is the energy and information center for clear seeing and clairvoyance. The sixth chakra contains information about seeing your own truth and distinguishing truth from lie. It allows you to see as spirit, clairvoyantly... to see energy.

The third eye also relates to seeing the whole picture without judgment. Issues which relate to blocks in the sixth chakra may include being blind to seeing the truth, intellectualizing but not really seeing, and limited judgmental thinking.

Seventh Crown Chakra. Located on top of the head at the crown. The seventh chakra is the energy center for higher spiritual information and knowingness. It gives you the ability to be balanced and know Truth. It gives you a direct connection to your own higher spiritual information and is a direct connection to God Source. The seventh chakra allows you-as-spirit to know things beyond what your mind could know.

The crown chakra relates to intuition and inspiration. Issues relating to blocks of the seventh chakra may include being disconnected from your own destiny. Dependence on leaders, gurus, or masters, may be an indication of a blockage.

Additional Chakras. There are seven primary chakras that are referenced when discussing the energy centers as just reviewed. In advanced spiritual chakra trainings, there are noted to be thirteen major chakra system and then minor chakras. The number can fluctuate based on various spiritual modalities and regions in the world. I am referencing two additional chakras beyond the seven major named the Braham and the Altman. Each are located outside of the body and noted below in the chart as one and two.

As I was writing this exercise God was very influential in its creation. I was trying to understand the relation of chakras and how they correlate to the divine. Further along you will note a table explaining the actual relationship in an organized fashion. It will provide you with a cohesive understanding.

Fruits of the Spirit

The Fruits of the Spirit are detailed within the Bible and further expanded through the dictionary. God/the Great Spirit very specifically showed me the alignment of each in relation to chakras, Angels, colors, earth elements, as well as types of people, animals and stones. Think about when you look at a rainbow and see the colors in perfect alignment. This correlates with the chakras in one's body.

Bible 1 Corinthians: 12

Gifts of the Holy Spirt

Love: Corinthians 12: 4-8
Joy: Galatians 5: 22-23
Wisdom: Acts 2:40
Knowledge: Mathew 10:19
Faith: John 20:30, 31
Healing: Mark 16:18
Miracles: Romans 15:19
Prophesy: Acts II: 28-30
Discerning of Sprits: 2 John: 9-11
Tongues: Acts 2: 4
Interpretation: I Corinthians 14: 5-19

There is direct correlation between the information provided and their relationship to each other. For this exercise the chakra's fall within nine categories. Please review the charts closely and don't hesitate to reference them again throughout the reading of this session or future reflections.

	GOD's GIFTS FRUITS GRACE SPIRITS	CHAKRAS	COLOR	ANIMAL	ELEMENT	SEED SOUNDS
1	Love Wisdom	Atman (outside of body)	Gold			
2	Joy Knowledge	Brahman (outside of body)	Silver			
3	Peace Faith, Wisdom	Crown Chakra top of head	White	Kachina	Magnetum	A
4	Patience Healings, Understanding Long Suffering	Third Eye Between eye brows	Purple	Archetypes all spirits living or dead	Radium	B
5	Kindness Working of Miracles Council	Throat Chakra throat	Blue	Human and Hierophant	Ether	G
6	Goodness Prophecy Power	Heart Chakra midway between breasts	Green	Mammals (4- legged)	Earth	F
7	Faithfulness Discerning of Spirits Knowledge	Solar Plexus In V shape of rib cage	Yellow	Birds	Air	E
8	Gentleness (different kinds of) Tongues Righteousness	Sakral Behind and below the navel	Orange	Aquatic Animals	Water	D
9	Self-control Interpretation of Tongues Divine Awfulness	Root Between base spine and pubic bone	Red	Snake	Fire	C

	PEOPLE	GEM-STONE	ANGEL	ASTRIAL PLANE	AURIC PLANE
3	Profit, Gurus, Saints	Diamond	Archangel Jophiel 2nd Ray - Sunday	Divine Plane	Casual Body or Ketheric Template
4	Spirit Teachers Spiritual Friends	Alexandrite	Archangel Raphael 5th Ray - Wednesday	Monadic Plane	Celestial Body
5	Religious leaders Divine rulers (Pope, Dali Lama, Karmapa)	Lapis/ Sapphire	Archangel Michael 1st Ray - Tuesday	Spiritual Plane	Etheric Template
6	Heart Chakra teachers (Jesus, Yogananda, Mother Theresa)	Emerald	Archangel Chamuel 3rd Ray - Monday	Intuitional Plane	Astral Body
7	Friends, Classmates Intellectuals, Politicians	Topaz/Peridot	Archangel Uriel 6th Ray - Thursday	Mental Plane	Mental Body
8	Teachers of feelings & who we share feelings with	Aquamarine	Archangel Gabriel 4th Ray - Friday	Emotional Plane	Emotional Body
9	Traditional roots relationships – family	Ruby	Archangel Zadkiel 7th Ray - Saturday	Physical Plane	The Etheric

The correlations within these charts was channeled information while writing this book. The next section we will go into a deeper study of word, emotions and what the fruits of the spirit are.

> **Love,** is a feeling of strong attachment induced by that which delights or commands admiration; preëminent kindness or devotion to another; affection; tenderness; as, the love of brothers and sisters.
>
> *"Of all the dearest bonds we prove Thou countest sons' and mothers' love Most sacred, most Thine own. (Amor, Aphrodite, Astarte, Benthamism, Christian charity, Christian love, Cupid, Eros, Freya, Kama, Love, Venus, accord, accordance, admiration, admire, adulate, adulation, affair, affinity, agreement, aim at, allegiance, altruism, amiability, amicableness, amity, amorousness, amour, angel)" Webster Dictionary*
>
> **Joy,** is the passion or emotion excited by the acquisition or expectation of good; pleasurable feelings or emotions caused by success, good fortune, and the like, or by a rational prospect of possessing what we love or desire; gladness; exhilaration of spirits; delight. (amusement, be in heaven, be pleased, beam, beatification, beatitude, bewitchment, blessedness, blissfulness, caper, caracole, carol, cheer, cheerfulness, chirp, chirrup, clap hands, cloud nine, crow, crow over, dance, delectation, die with delight, ecstasy, ecstatic, enchantment, enjoyment, exaltation, exhilaration, exuberance, exult, feel happy)
>
> **Peace**, is a state of quiet or tranquility; freedom from disturbance or agitation; calm; repose (Peace of God, accord, accordance, affinity, agape, agreement, amity, armistice, arrangement, array, assent, ataraxia, ataraxy, silence, bonds of harmony, breathing spell, brotherly love, buffer zone, caritas, cease-fire, cement of friendship, charity, chorus, coherence, coincidence, commodiousness, communion, community, community of interests)

Long Suffering, is bearing injuries or provocation for a long time; patient endurance of pain or unhappiness; patient; not easily provoked.

"The Lord God, merciful and gracious, long-suffering, and abundant in goodness and truth (enduring, patient)" Webster Dictionary

Kindness, is the state or quality of being kind, in any of its various senses; manifestation of kind feeling or disposition beneficence (act of grace, act of kindness, advantageousness, affability, agreeableness, aid, amiability, amicability, amicableness, amity, assistance, auspiciousness, benefaction, beneficence, beneficialness, benefit, benevolence, benignity, blessing, charitableness, charity, class, clemency, cogency, commiseration, compassion)

Goodness, is the quality of being good in any of its various senses; excellence; virtue; kindness; benevolence; as, the goodness of timber, of a soil, of food; goodness of character, of disposition, of conduct, etc. (Christianity, Christlikeness, Christliness, affability, affectionateness, agreeability, agreeableness, amenity, amiability, amicability, angelicalness, appropriateness, assured probity, beauty of holiness, beneficialness, benignancy, benignity, blamelessness, bliss, blissfulness, brotherhood, character, cleanness, compassion, compatibility, congeniality, cordiality, correctitude, correctness)

Faithfulness, is demonstrated through constancy, dedication, fidelity and loyalty.

Gentleness, is the quality or state of being mild, benevolent, docile, gentility; softness of manners, disposition and easygoingness.

Self-Control, is behaving with restraint exercised over one's self-command. (firmness, nerves, possession, presence of mind, resoluteness, resolution, resolve, self-command, self-possession, self-will, willpower)

Information referenced through *Bible* Galatians 5: 22, 23, *Webster Dictionary* and Derek Prince *The Gifts of the Spirit*.

This next area shows the relation of the Lord's Prayer in regards to Chakras.

The Lord's Prayer

Crown -	Our Father
Third Eye -	Who Art in Heaven
Throat -	Hallowed be Thy name
Heart -	Thy Kingdom Come, Thy will be done on earth as it is in heaven

Solar plexus -	Give us this day our daily bread
Navel -	And forgive us our trespasses as we forgive those who trespass against us
Root -	And lead us not into temptation but deliver us from evil
Brahman -	For Thine is the Kingdom, and the Power and the Glory forever and ever
Atman –	Amen

Information referenced through the *Bible* 1 Corinthians 12:4; The Lord's Prayer - Mathew 6: 9-11 and Spiritual Interpretation of Ashkhen Keshishian.

Auras

Auras are energy fields that envelop any living object or being. Aura colors can be seen with the eyes open. It can also be seen psychically with the eyes closed. It is best seen under soft light. Look beyond the object, and not focus on the object. Aura is observed more prominently around the hands, between the shoulders, neck and head. Those who see aura mostly observe the mental and etheric layers or planes. These are the colorful layers of the aura.

Etheric Layers or Planes

The etheric plane or etheric region is one of the planes of existence, or more specifically a subplane or planes, in esoteric philosophies, in some religious teachings and in New Age thought. In neo-Theosophical and Rosicrucian cosmology the etheric plane constitutes the fourth (higher) subplane of the physical plane, the lower three being the states of solid, liquid, and gaseous matter.

As noted by Theosophists C.W. Leadbeater and Annie Besant.

The most commonly known and used terms from the highest to the lowest planes as interpreted by Bonnie Moss are as follows:

DIVINE PLANE. Adi Plane or Plane of the Logos. Ketheric
MONADIC PLANE. Anupadaka Plane. Celestial- second spiritual.
SPIRITUAL PLANE. Atmic Plane. Etheric template first spiritual.
INTUITIONAL PLANE. Buddhic Plane. Higher mental.
MENTAL PLANE. Manasic Plane. Conscious mind.
EMOTIONAL PLANE. Astral Plane.
PHYSICAL PLANE. Physical Plane. Etheric.

These levels can be noted separately or in conjunction with each other. The colors are not physically separated by a line or space between them. They seem to fuse or change into one another.

One color may be more dominant than others. As one develops the ability to read aura, viable information can be derived from the different levels. There is no hierarchy of judgment involving the colors and their placement in the aura. The colors are only indicators of the person's current state can be read to strengthen the positive and/or help alleviate problems.

Remember, as living things change, so do the energy fields. As we develop, as we solve our problems and as we work through inhibiting blocks, we continue to balance our energies. They seem to fuse or change into one another. One color may be more dominant than others.

Seven Levels of Aura

Aura is a major energy field which surrounds the human body. Aura reflects the state of health, emotions, mind and spirituality. There are seven major auric layers known at this time. There is a symbiotic but interdependent relationship between your auric layers and the seven chakras of your body.

This is a photo of my Aura Chakra Report. This is a photo of my face and shows me to be INDIGO-BLUE. That is defined as calm, compassionate, nurturing, idealistic and peaceful. The diagram below is a full body color chart that also includes chakras and their colors. I had this report completed at the Daytona Metaphysical Book Store in Daytona Beach, Florida, however there are many reputable establishments where you can have yours taken if you desire. Please note that as each of us grow and develop or become overwhelmed by the world the colors will vary dependent upon where you are at that moment in time.

Auric Planes

The Etheric layer lies close to the human body approximately half an inch wide (1.3cms). It is usually grey, white or blue in color. Strong or weak health is revealed in this area. It is the most easily seen auric layer or etheric field.

This field can also be seen around trees, plants, animals, minerals, gems and even inanimate objects such as furniture. A white or black background will often highlight the etheric field for the naked eye to see.

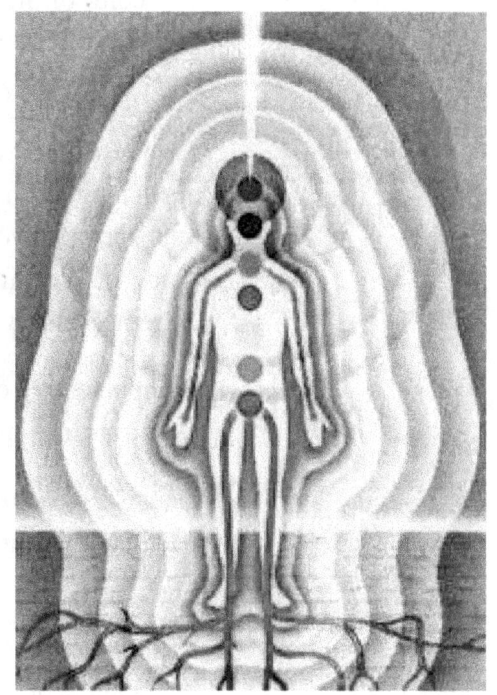

The Emotional body lies beyond the etheric field and extends to one to three inches (8cms) in a good state of health, it appears bright and colorful. These colors change as emotions change.

The Mental body lies beyond the emotional body. It is yellow, green or blue colors in good state of health. It relates to the thoughts and attitudes of the person.

The Astral body lies beyond the mental body. It shows an array of beautiful pastel colors such as pinks and blues when healthy and unblocked. It extends up to one foot (30cms.) from the body and indicates your capacity for conditional and unconditional love.

The Etheric template beyond the astral field is a type of x-ray or blueprint of the physical body. Illness or blocks, negativity can be observed and treated in this field. It extends one to two feet (60cms.) from the body. It is usually observed as grey/blue in color.

The Celestial body is the sixth auric field extending two to three feet (90cms.) from the body. It is filled with mother of pearl colors' and energies. It is the layer through which you can experience spiritual ecstasy.

The Causal body or Ketheric template is connected to the crown chakra. It is a type of photographic negative of the mental and spiritual aspects of the person. It is usually filled with golden shimmering light and is surrounded by a gold or silver halo or outer rim of protection. It extends from three feet to four feet (130cms.) outwards from the skin.

<u>Colors: What Colors Can Mean</u>

Colors are very important in our lives. They can assist in influencing mood, energy level and balance your emotions. We will review colors and what that are generally known to mean.

Gold	Indicates lots of spiritual energy, in tune with oneself. Muddy gold means one has not really come to terms with one's higher levels.
White	Is a very peaceful color and is known to elevate your vibration for healing work.

Purple	The color of intuition, a deeper purple hue shows a strong-willed and passionate person. It can also reflect intense erotic imagination and being over-bearing.
Blue	This comes in different shades. Gifted people have shades of blue in their aura. Intuitive people will show pale blue coloration within the purple bursting out like rays of sunshine, emanating from the heart outwards. A deeper blue can indicate loneliness. A very deep blue shows devotion, honesty and good judgment. Not all blues are positive. A muddier shade of blue indicates a domineering person with a tendency towards depression, or extreme sensitivity.
Green	Sympathetic to others, dependable and has healing abilities. Muddier shade could indicate jealousy- like "green with envy".
Yellow	Usually seen around a thinker, an analytical person. This could indicate a person in balance. Intelligent people show this color around their heads.
Orange	Bright orange means one is growing emotionally and paranormally. A dull shade means a person is unsure how to accept this growth. Muddy orange shows in a person with too much pride.
Red	A color of love or hate, strong emotions and a lot of energy. An intense red color, however, may indicate a person ready to fly off the handle.
Black	This is a confusing color. There is nothing wrong with black in one's aura. Black generally means one is shielding oneself from outside energies. This can also mean being unbalanced. One is hiding something or keeping secrets. A black ring around a child usually indicates some form of abuse. Adults who have not dealt with early abuse will carry this black ring until they are healed.
Brown	Indicates growth in a person. Seen around the head and with other colors emanating in combination, it indicates a person who is developing mentally, intuitively and organizing within. Brown by itself can indicate lack of energy, or one who has become "stagnant".
Gray	Indicates intuition and creativity, Silvery gray shows femininity while darker gray can mean secretiveness or physical imbalance. Gay men can show shades of gray in their aura.
Pink	The color of love, and honesty. It also depicts the quieter side of an artistic and creative person. Dark pink may indicate immaturity or changes with one's love life. Dull pink, however, watch out; Someone is lying.

Twinkling Lights	Presents like Christmas tree lights. A pregnant woman will show these lights in her aura. These lights could also mean one is going through some major and positive changes in life, usually seen in women.

NOTE: Colors are important aspect of aura reading: however, when non-physical energy combines with our body, it is confined to the limitations of density, light and form.

Seed Sounds

Sound vibrations correlate with the chart as each chakra vibrates at a different tone or frequency. The highest tone is located at the crown chakra which is on the top of your head. The tones then become lower as one moves down the chakras within the body. The lowest tone is noted at the base or root chakra. Sound can be used to assist in realigning or recharging your chakras. One method of this attunement is accomplished through the use of a tuning fork.

Energy work of Marlene Henkin, Mind-Body and Energy Therapy

Buddhist monks realign and balance their chakras through chanting. Native Americans use chanting and drumming for visioning and soul work also.

Gem Stones

People are naturally drawn to shinny and sparkling items such as gemstones. Often times they do not know why but actually all rocks and minerals hold a vibration and an energy tone that attracts them to specific pieces. There are thousands of precious and semi-precious gems that are sought after not only for the beauty but for the internal balance that is provided to person when it is worn.

Diamond or clear quartz is a symbol of purity. Its pure white light can help you to bring your life into a cohesive whole. It bonds relationships, bringing love and clarity into a partnership. Diamond is an amplifier of energy and one of the few stone that never needs charging. Mentally, diamond provides a link between the intellect and the higher mind. Diamond is the stone noted for the crown chakra.

Alexandrite is a stone of prosperity and longevity. It balances mind and emotions, pacifies soul and promotes spiritual growth. Alexandrite establishes harmony between physical, astral and mental bodies of the person, making its wearer more peaceful and compliant. Alexandrite strengthens creative abilities and fosters imagination. It may boost intuitive abilities, finding a way out from a desperate situation. Alexandrite opens and balances the third eye chakra.

Lapis or Sapphire opens and balances the throat chakra. Lapis Lazuli is a protective stone that contacts spirit guardians. Sapphire releases depression and spiritual confusion and stimulates concentration. It brings prosperity and attracts gifts of all kinds. Placed on the throat, Sapphire releases frustration and facilitates self-expression. This stone is a favorite for Edgar Casey.

Emerald is a stone of inspiration and infinite patience. Emerald opens the heart chakra and has a calming effect on the emotions. Emerald imparts mental clarity, strengthens memory, and inspires a deep inner knowing, truth, and aiding eloquent expression.

Topaz is a mellow, empathetic stone that directs energy to where it is needed most. It soothes, heals, stimulated, recharges, re-motivates, and aligns the meridians of the body. The vibrant energy of Topaz brings joy, generosity, abundance, and good health. It has traditionally been known as a stone of love and good fortune, bringing successful attainment of goals. Topaz promotes truth and forgiveness.

Peridot is a powerful cleanser. Releasing and neutralizing toxins on all levels, it purifies the subtle and physical bodies, and the mind. It opens, cleanses, and activates the heart and solar plexus chakras. These stones are used to open and enhance the Solar Plexus chakra.

Aquamarine. Aquamarine is a stone of courage. Its calming energies reduce stress and quiet the mind. Aquamarine has an affinity with sensitive people. It can invoke tolerance of others and overcomes judgmentalism, giving support to those overwhelmed by responsibility. The mineral clarifies perception, sharpens the intellect and clears confusion. It is useful for closure on all levels, and promotes self-expression. It can soothe fears and increase sensitivity, as well as sharpens intuition and clairvoyance. The gem is a wonderful for meditation. It shields the aura and aligns the chakras. (Caryl Haxworth)

Ruby. Ruby is an excellent stone for energy. Imparting vigor to life, it energized and balance but may sometimes overstimulate in delicate or irritable people. Ruby encourages passion for life but never in a self-destructive way. This stone is a powerful shield against psychic attack. Physically, Ruby overcomes exhaustion and lethargy and imparts potency and vigor. Conversely, it calms hyperactivity.

Colors as noted by Judy Hall from *The Crystal Bible*.

EXERCISE III: MEDITATION

The Fruits of the Spirit and Chakra Meditation

Find a quiet place to sit and relax. Be certain that all phones are shut off and that you will be uninterrupted for about ten minutes. Sit quietly and begin. Place your feet flat on the floor. You may feel more grounded, if you remove your shoes. Uncross your arms and legs and relax. Open yourself to this energy healing meditation. Close your eyes and take a deep breath. Breathe in and out slowly and with a cleansing intention. Inhale and exhale, releasing stress as you exhale. Inhale pure light and energy as you move into the mediation. Relax and be receptive to fully to absorb the light and brilliant energy of love that is entering into your body through your crown chakra.

As your breathing regulates, imagine yourself in perfect alignment. Look within and see the colors imagined within each chakra as vibrant and flowing in perfect harmony as created. You begin by calling in God's love and light. Open yourself to allow this pure love and light to flow into your body.

As you enter each chakra take a moment to feel the color, the pure movement, rotation and brilliance of each color and the powers of communication that are released within your body. You will be reciting the Lord's Prayer aligning phrases in conjunction with your chakra centers. Speak slowly, clearly and listen to all the syllables associated with each word. As you enter each chakra, allow the full love and light to enter into your being, slowly rotate and then to move through your essence.

Begin at the crown chakra and imagine a crystal clear white light entering the top of your head. You feel pure white light and love entering into your crown chakra. See the chakra then say, "Our Father"; *pause and experience.*

The white light travels slowly down to your third eye which is located along your brow line. This chakra is turning purple opening your intuition and insight with God and Angels "Who Art in Heaven"; *pause and experience.*

Draw the light lower to the throat chakra and watch as the violet fades to blue where we celebrate communication, "Hallowed be thy Name"; *pause and experience.*

The energy flows further down into the heart chakra where green is now prominent reflecting health, strength and Mother Earth "Thy Kingdom Come. Thy will be done on earth as it is in heaven"; *pause and experience.*

The light travels down to the solar plexus (V rib cage) where yellow radiates faithfulness, knowledge and air, "Give us this day our daily bread"; *pause and experience.*

The energy flows lower still and turns to brighten and become orange. This is the sacral chakra where gentleness and emotions are located. "Forgive us our trespasses as we forgive those who trespass against us"; *pause and experience.*

The energy moves lower and the color radiates and pulses red at the root chakra. This chakra supports the fire and self-control "And Lead us not into temptation but deliver us from evil"; *pause and experience.*

All chakras and colors within your body are rotating and pulsating in perfect alignment; *pause and experience.*

Now you travel outside of the body and silver now radiates around your body celebrating Joy "For Thine is the Kingdom, and the Power and the Glory forever and ever"; *pause and experience.*

The silver is then transformed into gold, pure and glistening gold. Shimmering wisdom and love completing the essence of our being, "Amen"; *pause and experience.*

It is time to come back now. All your chakras are in perfect alignment. You are moving back and floating into your chair, into the room once again and into your body comfortably seated in this time and space. Wiggle your fingers and toes and open your eyes when you feel ready. Welcome home once again. Take a few minutes to write down what you experienced.

EXERCISE IV: SELF REFLECTION

Take your time writing and reflecting on the experience that you just had. Write any and all details even if they don't make logical sense to you. There are all pieces of your puzzle that will come together as you develop.

What did you see?

_____
_____
_____
_____
_____

What did you feel?

_____
_____
_____
_____
_____

What did you hear?

_____
_____
_____
_____
_____

What did you experience?
_____
_____
_____
_____
_____

Note to self:
_____
_____
_____
_____
_____
_____

EXERCISE V: HOMEWORK

Chakras are your personal energy centers. Be mindful of this and envision that each of your energy centers is like a pin wheel that slowly turns. If we feel stuck it is often found that at least one wheel has stopped turning. When you are feeling overwhelmed or out of balance take a few minutes to mentally envision each of your chakras. Start at the top of your head and move through the colors and locations and then focus your energy to see them all turning in alignment at the same speed.

_____
_____
_____
_____
_____
_____
_____

For best results plan for one lesson at each session.

PERSONAL DEVELOPMENT THROUGH SELF EXPLORATION

Lesson 4: Carrying the Weight of the World on Your Hips

EXERCISE I: INTRODUCTION

This lesson was very ironic for me as I have spent my life within this struggle and definitely not on the winning side. This is the title I was given so this is the lesson that I will share. Because this has been such a personal issue for me the only thing that seems appropriate is to start with me, and the challenges and ghosts that chase me.

I have always been an overachiever. Personally, I call myself a triple "AAA" personality. A singular "A" just doesn't seem to properly reflect my scope. The overachieving is specific thought to whatever I am focused on at the time. That focus changes periodically and is always passionately driven exponentially at warp speed.

I strive for approval and positive reinforcement. It seems to be the driving force behind everything I attempt. I have ridiculous standards for myself that no one could achieve and therefore I create a pool of self-destructive behaviors that have taken me years to comprehend and resolve.

EXERCISE II: INFORMATION

Personal Development

I am a middle child and was very sickly as a young girl because of being an asthmatic. Dealing with the illness prior to proper medications being invented such as inhalers and limited research on how to treat asthma. I was also plagued with a long list of allergies that continually instigated the asthma attacks. It was very difficult to manage the ailment. Therefore, with a few siblings and a busy life, I remember riding in the back of the car with a bucket going to wherever on a regular basis. An asthmatic can't breathe because the bronchial tubes are inflamed and very little air can flow through the lungs, so the body automatically tries to reject any foreign items that may be clogging the passage. We lived in a rural setting in New Hampshire, on top of a hill in a lovely modest home. Mom stayed home and Dad was manager of a local grocery store.

Dad's dream was to open his own business, so when he found an old restaurant with an apartment downstairs in another town, we moved. It was a neighborhood that didn't welcome this change. Never experiencing animosity, this was a new experience for an eight year old with a limited perception of life. The restaurant/apartment complex was in dire need of renovation. It has been abandoned ten plus years earlier. The past owner had just locked the doors and left the tables set for the next day, food in the coolers and dry goods stored. Every creature in the neighborhood had set up housekeeping in this storehouse of abundance.

My parents were both working very hard and long hours to make this venture successful, but as this wasn't supported by the community it was an uphill battle. For me, I remember spending much time alone. The neighborhood kids were mean and didn't like any of us, but they liked that I could get free food so I was exploited. I remember eating a box of mini peanut butter cups and they made me feel better.

It is interesting as I get older, I can be a little more reflective and spend more time exploring the roots of this personality trait. We all have stories but the ending is the same. We find ourselves in a never ending unhealthy relationship with food that drives our lives.

The battle of weight maintaining a healthy weight can be a lifelong process where you have spent years with a closet full of various size clothes to match the programs and pills that you have tried to magically conquer the ongoing battle. How many times have you joined me in saying?

> I am starting on Monday …..

> Today is the first day of …..

> I will never again …..

Only to find yourself slowly slipping into the same self-destructive pattern of food pacification once again. Why can't I get off this wheel? Why don't I have enough self-control? What void is food filling within me? How can I just stop?

Another side note of information that I recently discovered within myself which specifically correlates to this battle is what type of psychic sensitive you fall within. My primary gift is Clairsentience which is when you are feeling or sense other's experiences and emotions. When you fall within this category you can experience emotional overload and may have a difficult time being around large crowds and may turn to food to help curb or suppress all the feelings that swirl around you on a daily basis. Let's take a few minutes to explore some basic concepts in human behavior:

Animals and plants are created to adapt to the conditions of the habitats in which they live

> **What is adaptation?** It is a way an animal's body helps it survive, or live, in its environment. Humans are not exempt from these same natural survival intuitions, and at the foundation of life's essential needs, wants, and desires, subconscious animal instincts are the driving force for every action of the human being. Some of the most basic animal instincts identified include safety, food, sleep and the emotions of love, pleasure, anger, and fear which all seem to remain consistent among all animals. Human nature is directly related to animal instincts in that all societies develop their own standards of behavior typically based on the best possible way to fill each member's essential needs.

Take a minute to consider these animals and how they have natural defense capabilities: crab, crayfish, snail, scallop, lobster, shrimp, mussel, barnacle, oyster, clam, turtle, armadillo, ladybug, porcupine, eagle, lion, bear, wild boar, hawk, skunk, gorilla or opossum as a few examples. God has provided the creatures with natural protection or barriers such as teeth, horns, shells, quills or talons for self-preservation.

Now let's look at humans. We are totally reliant upon others to provide us with our basic needs of food, shelter and protect us from a world of evils for many years until we are capable to care for ourselves and leave the nest. All too often we leave with far more baggage than is necessary which accumulated during this period. The good news is that we survived!

What role has food played in your life? A friend can lift you up, acts as a companion when you are bored or lonely, is a partner for celebrating, calming if you are anxious, and even is adaptive for protection? Food is necessary as a basic fuel for our body's survival. A healthy diet with exercise are essential for proper system functioning.

Gaining weight is a way to disappear in the world. Some extra weight takes the focus off of you when other humans are constantly on the prowl seeking to mate. There are many reasons that you may have needed this protection but let's look at the probability that you are using food to fill the void in your life.

You have spent your life learning to bury old hurts and have either never truly learned how to become worthy or lost it through the years. We seek others approval as ours isn't enough. We repeatedly hurt ourselves through food because we believe we deserve it or we just can't stop the cycle of the love/hate or mind/soul relationship of self.

The only true answer to stop this cycle is deep within our souls. We must take the time and energy to feel and experience the emotions locked within and to understand that **it is normal have and feel emotions!** To be human is to experience love, hate, anticipation, anger, fear, jealousy, exhaustion, excitement, lust, joy, boredom, passion, admiration, comfort and anxiety.

The second chakra is correlated to food, weight and self-satisfaction directed through emotion. It is represented by the color orange. It is the second, sacral plexus chakra. From the red root we move into a more sophisticated stage of creativity. The second chakra is the foundation of the emotional body, it influences our ability to feel emotions, sensations and atmospheres, and controls our ability to release our emotions. In silky waves of orange we become aware of our physical beings and begin to make prime connections to the magnificence of our bodies. Orange speaks to us about exploration. New additives are mixed with raw matter, and this is where spirit and physical unite. When the chakra is performing correctly a person will feel healthy and balanced. Through this alignment, we experience intuition, a good frame of mind, energy and success.

EXERCISE III: MEDITATION

Weight of the World

Find a quiet place to sit and relax. Be certain that all phones are shut off and you will be uninterrupted for about ten minutes. Sit quietly and start. Find some background music soft and gentle to set a meditative tone. Slow down and take several deep cleansing breaths in and out. Sit straight with your hands in your lap and feet flat on the ground. With each breath try to relax and more and more- in and out, in and out. Let your body become loose, feel the stressing and tightness just float away. Try to quiet your mind. Slow it down. Let the thoughts clear away, when one comes in gently release it with blessings to return if necessary at another time. Deep breath in and then out once more.

A white light is gently flowing down and enfolds you. You are filling with peace, love and protection as we move forward. Ask your Higher Power to hear the information and guidance that is being sent.

Just sit and listen quietly to your surroundings and to the soothing music. Begin to observe how you and your body feel. Gently place thoughts, information and ideas that you want to remember in your memory bag to take out when this exercise is over.

Acknowledge your body and its voice. Take a deep breath and release the stress. Feel the sensations that you are experiencing at this moment. Envision a soothing orange energy moving into and surrounding your solar plexus. With each thought, pause and stay in that space for a few seconds and feel the orange rotating in your solar plexus.

- Feel the orange energy. Listen to the energy as it swirls though your body and balances once again.
- "Hear" – Ha-ah is exhale sound. Hear your soul.
- How is food related?
- What is food filling in your life?
- What are your emotions?
- How do you feel about having emotions?
- Is it ok to feel different emotions?
- Hear your higher power and your guides.
- What are they saying?
- What is the orange telling you?
- What are you feeling?
- Feel frustration.
- Feel comfort.

- Feel fear.
- Feel peace.
- Feel sorrow.
- Feel joy.
- Feel loneliness.
- Feel the unbounding Love of God.
- Feel acceptance for the perfect being that you are.
- Be still and know your heart.
- Listen with your spirit and soul …..

It is time to slowly return. Take a breath in and out, back to the room, back to your seat, back into your body. Thank your Higher Power for this time. Deeply breathe in and out. Wiggle your feet and fingers then open your eyes when you feel ready and refreshed.

EXERCISE IV: SELF REFLECTION

Take a few minutes and write down what you just experienced. They don't need to make sense but capture the experience for later evaluation.

What did you see?

_____
_____
_____
_____
_____

What did you feel?

_____
_____
_____
_____
_____

What did you hear?

_____
_____
_____
_____
_____

What did you experience?

_____
_____
_____
_____
_____

Notes to Self:

_____
_____
_____
_____
_____
_____
_____

EXERCISE V: HOMEWORK

Forgiveness Exercise: Free yourself <u>Now</u>!

Forgiveness simply is a way of freeing your spirit and becoming an unlimited being. Peacefulness, increased energy is the prize and forgiveness is the price.

Take a forgiveness inventory. Write down the name of every being, living or deceased, who has irritated, hurt or with whom you have unfinished business. Most people will have three or four pages and <u>your name</u> needs to be included.

Release and forgive. In a solitary room, go down the list and one name at a time, hold the image of each person in your mind and tell him/her, "I forgive you and I release you. I hold no forgiveness back. My forgiveness is total. I am free and you are free". Be sure to complete the entire list.

Complete nightly releases. Every evening take a mental inventory of the day and activities - is there anyone you need to forgive? Bless them on their journey. It is important to release and cleanse the consciousness on a daily basis so that resentment isn't accrued.

_____
_____
_____
_____
_____

For best results plan for one lesson at each session.

Lesson 5: The Spirit of Love

EXERCISE I: INTRODUCTION

It's all about acceptance, gratitude and understanding. The goal is liking then loving who and what you are. Tap into your universal love of self.

This lesson was created for Valentine's Day, but it is applicable to each and every day. This is a day created to celebrate love. Love truly is a double edged sword. Divine love is the only thing that never changes. Connection to Source has no conditions! God *is* love. "I am that I am" (Exodus 3:14). This also is a day if you are single many become more sensitive and may feel alone, lonely, rejected and incomplete as you may not feel as though you match the rest of society. This is your ego playing with your mind. According to Eckhart Tolle, the reason why the romantic special love relationship is such an intense and universally sought-after experience is that it seems to offer liberation from a deep-seated state of fear, need, lack and incompleteness that is part of the human ego condition in its unredeemed and unenlightened state. There is a physical as well as a psychological dimension to this state. Physically, you are not a whole, nor will you ever be. It takes both the male and female to create entirety of self, and there lies the crux of human dilemmas of love or so some believe. God has made each of us perfect as we are!

EXERCISE II: INFORMATION

Being My Valentine. My means yourself, take time to love who you are just as you are. Love is always around you, grasp it, hold it and accept it to be true and just for you!

BE You were born a human **be**ing not a human **do**ing – try to sit and "be".

M **Make** your own choices don't let life choose for you.

Life is in continual motion: rotating on its axis; changing seasons; ticking clocks; a rising and setting of the sun and moon – one of the only things that is guaranteed in life is that it will change and human nature is to continually try and keep things the same. An impossible mission in life!

Y **You** are created perfectly as God intends.

There is no other or has there ever been another person who is exactly as you are. Had the same experiences, lived as you have. It is the same with a snowflake there are no two the same. No one has your exact handprint or finger print. You are unique and special!

What delights you, is pleasurable to you?

What gives you joy?

What makes you smile?

What makes you laugh?

What motivates you?

What are you passionate about?

What did you dream of as a child?

What do you dream about today?

What do you want to dream about for the tomorrows?

V   To **Value** something is to invest much of your time and worldly resources. Your time, talent, knowledge, resources, strength, communication, creativity, core personal values and beliefs.

A   **Acceptance** of self – Why are we so easy to forgive others and have such a difficult time forgiving ourselves? You are human – ever growing, learning and changing. You are perfect in God's eye exactly as you are! You are a perfect being created of God's love and are a light unto all that you come into contact with. It is critical to remember that unrest in the mind can manifest itself into physical challenges. Therefore one must take time to stop, evaluate where you are on a regular basis and allow for forgiveness of self. You must understand the perfection of your divine path on this earth-plane classroom.

L   **Love** of self – reflect God's unconditional love. The love of your body, your mind, uniqueness, your talents, your own individuality and beautiful perspective of life.

E   **Engage** – in life sharing your gifts and talents is serving. How do you know that you can't if you have never tried?

N   **New** – beginnings keep you younger, fresh, energized, thinking clearer, excited and exhilarated. As Oprah Winfrey states, "You can start fresh every day."

T   **Transform** – if you want something changed in your life do it, learn it, live it, be it – Go for it! You are the only one who can make the transformation of self. Life is waiting for you to make the transformation.

I   **Inspire** – follow what inspires you!
Follow your true spiritual self and be your own best Valentine. What makes your blood roar, excites you, drives your passion, take time to really see what that is. Inspire and be inspired.

N   **Now** – why do we wait for tomorrow when today just keeps passing by. It is said "the greatest gift in the world is the present". Come with me. Why don't you open it today?

E   **Exemplify** – by being the best that you can in all things! By doing your best you will always live celebrating God! You will be satisfied and confident to move to the next level of life.

EXERCISE III: MEDITATION

The Spirit of Love

Find a quiet place to sit and relax. Be certain that all phones are shut off and you will be uninterrupted for about ten minutes. Sit quietly, close your eyes and begin to quiet your thoughts, breathing slowly in and out. Sit in a comfortable position with your feet on the ground and hands up in your lap. Breathe in, filling your lungs and keep filling until you feel it all the way into your soul – now slowly release the breath, exhale – exhale – exhale until you are totally empty. Now slowly inhale and exhale allowing your mind to just be. Relax your body, your mind and your thoughts with each breath. When thoughts enter, bless them and release them into the winds while you continue to breathe and relax deeper with each breath.

You are sitting completely relaxed letting all other thoughts gently float away. Your body feels light and you are in peace, warm beautiful peace. You can hear your heart beat, and feel the pulse of your blood as it flows through your body, moving to all areas providing the life and energy needed by every cell.

Now imagine a large ball of pink light. It is a soft pink and in motion. The colors of pink are waving and swirling around this beautiful pink sphere. You can see into the pink light and know that it is filled with love, God's love, Universal love. Watch as this beautiful pink sphere of pure love gently rotates. The peace, joy, pure essence of acceptance and unconditional love is within this pink ball. You now see that the ball is expanding, growing before your eyes, getting larger and larger. The swirling of pink love is still rotating around. It has grown so large that the edges of the ball have moved over you and you find yourself within this beautiful pink sphere.

You look around and admire all the waves and swirls of love: kind friendly love, a neighbor running a quick errand for you; love of chocolate and flavors of life that bring you joy; the love of people… classmates… work peers… acquaintances… strangers who open a door and gift you with a good wish and a smile for the day. The love of nature in the world surrounds you - the warm sun, the cool evenings, the sparkling stars above, the mysterious moon and curious craters within. God's gift of life- birds, squirrels, cats, dogs, wildlife are all around. The love from mother earth, the ground that we stand upon and life that stabilizes our existence and embraces you. You feel the love from water – the cool refreshing rebirth after plunging in and out, a light rain, a swim, a long hot shower; whispering winds as the love from air moves through the trees softly caressing your skin. You hear the sound as it magically touches your soul through vibration and movement. Smell, as memories and fragrances are felt though your nasal cavity during an inhale; taste the feelings and emotions that come from various flavors and textures as they move over your pallet. Glorious love and unconditional acceptance from Father God the Great Spirit, the love of family... mother... father... brother... sister... aunts... uncles... grandparents... children a daughter... a son... grandchildren... great-grandchildren; a husband or wife... your life partner... and dearest friends who become family through the heart of love.

The love of all is swirling in and around you, coursing through your body, your blood, bones, muscles all areas within and outside of your body. This beautiful pink unconditional love from all is filling and re-nourishing every cell and ion within your existence: mentally, physically, emotionally and spiritually. You are completely filled and renewed by this all-encompassing love from the universe. Bask in the glory and let the love just pulse and vibrate though your being ... the oneness of love within and without.

(Pause ...)

Your body is now filled, complete rejuvenated and the pink ball of light is gently fading and rising above to move beyond. Just be ... Take a moment and bask in the glory of the gift of love.

Start to come back now. Take a deep breath in and out, once again breathing deeply. Feel the seat beneath you. Feel the room around you. Take another large breath, in and out and slowly open your eyes when you feel ready.

EXERCISE IV: SELF REFLECTION

What did you see?

_____
_____
_____
_____
_____

What did you feel?

_____
_____
_____
_____
_____

What did you hear?

_____
_____
_____
_____
_____

What did you experience?

_____
_____
_____
_____
_____

Love is a powerful gift that is showered upon us each and every day. Please accept this gift. You are worthy of this gift. You can share this gift. You are a Gift!

You are made perfect, by God, You are Devine perfection – just as you are.

Notes to self:

_____
_____
_____
_____
_____
_____
_____

EXERCISE V: HOMEWORK

Make a list: things that you want to do, places to go, experiences you want to see, to taste, to feel, to smell, to accomplish, to explore, to learn, to play, to be, what do you want?

_____
_____
_____
_____

Try something new – think about what lays deep inside as a desire and do it! No criticism or judgment just celebrate your adventure of self. Create your list now!

_____
_____
_____
_____
_____

What would you like to change about yourself? Think of three ways you might be able to accomplish that change. Remember there are no boundaries in ideas, boundaries are only created by a mind or man.

_____
_____
_____
_____
_____

What makes your blood roar? What excites you? What brings you pleasure? What makes you warm? What makes you feel loved?

_____
_____
_____
_____
_____

For best results plan for one lesson at each session.

Lesson 6: A True Warrior in Today's World

EXERCISE I: INTRODUCTION

This lesson is very close to my heart. As we age and grow in our understanding of the greater existence beyond, you will find that some things in nature call to your soul. You may not be sure what the reasoning is for the attraction but you feel its strength and know of the connected power beyond your understanding. As I started this journey, there has been a greater calling towards Native American ways of life. It truly comes down to a better understanding of Mother Earth, her natural powers and respect for her while we are on this earth plane.

As we move through each day we encounter so many people, situations, and events that guide or influence our lives. It is so easy to get caught up in the moments of emotion and ride off into the sunset with spontaneous reactions. This becomes a vicious cycle of emotional energy that can create a wild rollercoaster ride and you may have a very difficult time getting off. Gathering attachments to past issues clogs our channels to the Divine. It is much more challenging to stop, take a few minutes to digest the information or situation and rationalize what has taken place and move forward more clearly on a solid path.

EXERCISE II: INFORMATION

Spiritual Warrior. The purpose of this lesson is to understand the meaning of being a Spiritual Warrior in the world today. The following topics will be discussed:

- Great Spirit & You
- Origin of your Roots
- Finding Peace
- Honoring Mother Earth
- Positive Power
- Fullness of Nature
- Finding Strength in the World Around You
- Finding Strength Within Your Soul

Let's begin this journey by examining some basic definitions as they relate to your personal experiences from *Webster's Dictionary*.

Warrior
One who is engaged aggressively or energetically in an activity, cause, or conflict. A man engaged or experienced in warfare, a soldier. A person engaged in some struggle or conflict. A person who has shown great vigor, courage, or aggressiveness.

Courage
The state or quality of mind or spirit that enables one to face danger, fear, or vicissitudes with self-possession, confidence, and resolution; bravery.

Strength
The quality or state of being strong; bodily or muscular power vigor. Mental power, force; moral power, firmness, or courage. Power by reason of influence, authority, resources, numbers.

After examining these definitions, let's reflect on the personal meanings of the words. Jot down any thoughts.

How do the following specific areas resonate to your warrior mentality or soul?

Family – individual members, family position, expectations, individuality, fear, or perhaps wanting a family of your own.

_____
_____
_____
_____
_____

Employment – your job, a career, and peers within, personalities, power plays, satisfaction, expression and growth options.

_____
_____
_____
_____
_____

Finances – the never-ending balancing of earning and expenses, uncontrolled life changes which can dramatically impact financial decisions.

_____
_____
_____
_____
_____

Survival on earth and natures elements – climate, weather events, urban locations, surroundings, and safety issues.

_____
_____
_____
_____
_____

Education – school, teachers, life experiences, self-initiatives.

_____
_____
_____
_____
_____

Self - personal calling, individuality, aspirations, dreams, core beliefs, confidence, strength, anger, courage, frustration, happiness, fears, seed of personality.

_____
_____
_____
_____
_____

Religion – basic belief in a higher power, what have we been taught, experienced and finding peace within your soul.

_____
_____
_____
_____
_____

Life is school and is meant to have challenges. Your intellect creates the intensity of the battles. Conflict is just that, a situation that makes you feel uncomfortable. It may not fit within your timing, morals, values, emotion or personal priority. It is much easier to look at each situation on its own; however, it is also helpful to review for possible patterns. In the midst many challenges it can feel overwhelming at times, but once broken down and evaluated it is truly much more manageable. The key is to try and to look at the situation as a third party without all the emotions that may cloud your perception and decision process.

You have reviewed your challenges and now it is important to identify your reservoir for renewal. We are born as beings of love and light, created from energy that strengthens our souls encourages Divine Purpose.

Note: Conflict and duality between mind and higher (ego) self creates suffering (Buddha).

Where do you to find peace?
___
___
___
___
___

Where do you find strength?
___
___
___
___
___

Where in nature do you feel at home, a great sense of connection, belonging, and one with Mother Earth?
___
___
___
___
___

What makes you happy, creates laughter, encourages love and lightens your heart?
___
___
___
___
___

Warrior Walk

As a warrior in the world today it is important to have the necessary tools available to fill you with the strength and courage that is needed from time to time. Mother Earth provides us with many wonderful gifts that naturally provides each of us with peace, power, protection and presence of perfection. This gift can be created by each of you in the form of a Walking Stick. This is a perfect time to create your personal walking stick. This stick will be a blending of your energy along with the natural items and gifts from Mother Earth. Together the energies will link into a synchronized vibration. This stick will provide you with guidance, support, protection and inspiration as you walk in this world.

Gather your natural craft items. You will need a walking stick as your base. Perhaps you can go out and find one or maybe one has already found you. Collect items such as: shells, feathers, acorns, pinecones, crystals, stones, raw hide and leather strips, so they are easily accessible to build your walking stick.

Take a break from the book and take your experience outside. You may have your stick and some supplies already but you will need to go out and spend time with nature to find a few more. Mother Earth is calling you to come and visit, to go out for a walk. Pause to feel… to listen… to look…to smell. Bring your walking stick with you as you explore. In this exercise it is very important to use all your senses and experience this meditation as intended! Walk around and collect what is calling to you. Be sure engage your hearing during this process as words and messages float into your consciousness. Write down these messages and corresponding feelings at this time to reflect upon later.

Create Your Stick

It's time to create your Walking Stick. You have collected all types of items. Lay them out across the table. As you spread your items out, as your heart will direct you what to use on your stick. It is time to begin, so let your creativity flourish. You can tie on items with twine, leather, wrap items, glue on items, and carve out designs. Follow your inner guidance. There is no right or wrong. This stick is a physical manifestation or representation of Mother Nature blending with your soul and your spiritual journey. Take your time. You may work on it awhile and then set it down and return and add more. Work with your stick until you feel as if it is completed. Your creation may evolve over time as you grow in the light.

Once your Walking Stick is completed than it is time to continue this lesson. First take a few minutes to look at your stick. Truly feel it, the pride and powerful gift that it is! Take time to note the types of natural items, animals and or stones, which have personal meaning for you. We will be entering into the meditation. Be sure to hold your Walking Stick. It is time to fully connect to the power that it possesses.

EXERCISE III: MEDITATION

A Warrior Within

Find a quiet place to sit and relax. Be certain that all phones are shut off you will be uninterrupted for about ten minutes. Uncross your arms and legs, sit up straight and be comfortable. Place your Walking Stick between your legs or across your lap. Quiet yourself. Slow down and take several deep cleansing breaths in and out with each breath try to relax more and more. In and out, in and out. Close your eyes, relax let your body become loose, feel the stress and tightness just float away. Try to quiet your mind, slow it down. Let the thoughts clear away, when one comes in gently release it with blessings to return if necessary at another time. Breathe deeply in and then out once more.

A White Light is gently coming down through your crown chakra. This white light is flowing through you and is now surrounding you and your Walking Stick. The white light is slowing filling you with peace, love and protection as we move forward.

It is time to travel to your sacred space. We all have a space outside in nature that is our own special place to "just be". It is a natural space where you find peace, tranquility and a connection to the Great

Spirit. Let's travel there now. Perhaps your place is sitting on a bench at your favorite park. Maybe you have gone to the shoreline and find a secluded space and settle by the sea. Perhaps you find yourself sitting upon a high bluff watching the world below. You might find a soft space to settle in a field of flowers or in the middle of a soft green forest, near a stream, in a small boat floating on a pond. Travel in your mind's eye to that special place in nature where the world fades away and you can sit and feel Mother Earth as she reaches out to you to fill you with her knowledge that is endless and eternal though the centuries before and after.

Be still and listen quietly to your surroundings, to the soothing sounds of the earth. You may hear the chattering of nearby squirrels, a melody from a bird, and the whisper of the winds as a light breeze passes by, the sound of water flowing or the crest and fall of each welcoming wave. Listen to life - the beautiful earthly music that enfolds you as you sit in your most favorite, peaceful, beautiful space upon this earthly planet. What is Mother Earth speaking to you? Hear her transference of knowledge.

Your senses become attuned to your surroundings. You feel the sun upon your face, a soft breeze, the firm surface that sturdily holds your weight securely upon this earth plain. Maybe you feel fog gently settling around you or snowflakes as they so delicately fall upon and around you, the moisture of rain - a cleansing of water from Great Spirit's hands washing away the sins of mankind to begin anew. Sit in peace and feel. Feel each element of your surroundings. Mother Earth is radiating from your heart. Feel the divine connection of this moment.

Take a deep breath. What do you smell? Perhaps you inhale the freshness of greenery, or the soft perfume of surrounding flowers. Do you smell salt from the sea or moisture as the rain begins to fall. Do you smell the season? Is there a briskness in the air as autumn approaches and a frost as it nips in the air? You may smell Mother Earth – her pure earthen essence of where you sit. Do you smell a tree? Is there a freshness of evergreen or perhaps cocoa from swaying palms? Relax in this moment and breathe. Breathe in Mother Earth and what she is telling you and your Walking Stick.

You are now connected to the rhythm of Mother Earth's Heart. Listen and feel the aroma of life and the knowledge that is being shared though the gift of smell. Open your mouth slightly and inhale deeply. What do you taste? Is it sweet, wet, dry, bitter, silky, soft or sour? Listen to your taste buds what are they telling you? What does the Great Spirit want you to taste in this life? Taste and remember this moment.

Open your mind's eye. Look around you in this most beautiful peaceful place what do you see? What is it that the Great Spirit wants you to see, don't only look on the outside and the sacred place where you sit, but also within. Look within the golden white light of infinite knowledge, strength, truth and courage what do you see?

Perhaps there are shapes, colors, symbols, loved ones, spirit beings, angels, guides or your ultimate source in this life. What do you see... Take mental notes... Within and without...

What is the knowledge that Mother Earth wants you to see both within yourself and your existence? Cherish this moment and the gift of Divine Vision.

Savor this wonderful presence of being, listening, feeling, smelling, tasting and seeing all of what Mother Earth wants you to know in this life as you move forward on your journey. Gather the thoughts, information and ideas that you want to remember gently place in your memory bag to take with you when this experience is over.

Now it is time to slowly make your way back to the Earth plane. Take a breath in and out. You are now leaving your most sacred space. Before you go please take a moment and say thank you. Thank any and all spirit beings, guides, loved ones, Mother Earth, Father God and the Great Spirit for all their earthly and eternal knowledge that they have so generously shared with you on this day.

It is time to come back, back to this space, back to this room, and back to your seat. Feel the chair beneath you. Feel your Walking Stick in your hand. Begin to move your fingers and toes, Ground your physical presence. Take a deep breath in and out and open your eyes slowly as you settle back in the here and now.

EXERCISE IV: SELF REFLECTION

Take a moment and stretch. With paper and pen, please take notes of what has been gifted to you on this day:

- Where did you go?
  _____
  _____

- Where do you find your strength?
  _____
  _____

- Where do you find peace?
  _____
  _____

- Where do you find guidance?
  _____
  _____

- Where do you find love?
  _____
  _____

- Where do you find Grace?
  _____
  _____

- Where do you find courage?
  _____
  _____

- Where do you find satisfaction?
  _____
  _____

- Where do you find joy?
  _____
  _____

- Where do you want to be?
  _____
  _____

We are all what and who we want to be nature is all interconnected with Universal Knowledge. You just need to set your intent. You are the warrior of your world and there are no battles, only experiences and lessons in life to be learned and shared. You travel now with a kindred spirit that is your Walking Stick into your future.

What did you see?
_____
_____
_____
_____
_____

What did you feel?
_____
_____
_____
_____
_____

What did you hear?
_____
_____
_____
_____
_____

What did you experience?

___

This has been a very powerful chapter and opportunity to learn much about yourself. The information that is being gathered is like a quilt. Some pieces are bold and easy to identify while others seem as if they are fractured and confusing. Be patient with yourself. This is a workbook where you are exploring deep within to get a better understanding of who you are and who you want to become. Take the time to really explore this information as you hold the key to all which is locked deep within. Review your answers as they become new beginnings. You may want to journal to see your growth as you walk your path with your new Walking Stick.

Notes to self:

___

EXERCISE V: HOMEWORK

Do some research on what you have added to your Walking Stick? Native Americans understand that each animal is known as a totem and they each have power or knowledge that is unique to each. Take a few minutes and look on line for Native American Totems and name the animal that was used on your stick. Learn the lessons that have been gifted to you. Remember leather also comes from an animal generally a deer. Feathers are from specific birds, or perhaps you have added a shell or bone. Remember these are honored gifts who are now blessing your with their powers and special meaning to <u>you</u>.

___

For best results plan for one lesson at each session.

CONNECTING WITH MOTHER EARTH TO BUILD YOUR SPIRITUALITY

Mother Earth is alive! She is one with all spiritual beings and showcased through Great Spirit. Living energies are intertwined within this earth plane. We will now explore new ways for each of you to tap into your own unique selves. The power of Mother Earth is in constant motion and changes through alignment of the planets, the seasons, the moon and sun phases as well as your physical location. Are you on a mountain top, perhaps on a shoreline? Elevation and geographic location along with mineral substances all can play a role in this self- communication. Let's begin your new adventure. Lie on the earth and feel her heartbeat. There is a natural interconnected rhythm.

Lesson 7: Drumming

EXERCISE I: INTRODUCTION

Drumming is a way to connect with Mother Earth. It is a sacred way to tap into the very roots of your existence. Each beat sends a natural vibration into Her soul though Her very essence.

EXERCISE II: INFORMATION

The drum is primal as is the art of drumming. Our bodies cry and long for the steady rhythm of balance of male/female energies. Centering and connecting to Source in healing ourselves and others. Our bodies function to the pattern and energy expelled in waves that are being transmitted within the drumming. Our bodies naturally align with the beating, the heart falls in line, the flow of blood pulsing through our veins and organs all follow the natural rhythm of each beat.

Our bodies are made of millions of cells. Within each cell, we are in a state of constant vibration. Therefore, music and vibration of tone can be very important to spiritual development.

When time is taken to drum, no words are needed. It is at this nonverbal level of communication pulsing through Mother Earth that realigns the chaos of energies in the world in which we live. The drumming calls in spirits of all kinds, such as the animals who have sacrificed skins to become the drum that is being used at this time. It could be goat spirit or perhaps cow spirit who is showcased within your drum, its skin pulled tightly to create a firm sound. This is why every drum has a unique voice and soul. The steady rhythm provides a low and calming vibration that attracts all species of spirit to come forth and experience in a minuscule moment in time.

When drumming vibration is near, the body feels the call prior to the ears actually hearing the sounds that are being omitted. The vibration is felt within your soul which begins to search towards what is pulsing and drawing you in. Then you begin to hear the steady rhythm of the beating drum and move towards it to listen with your total being to what is being spoken to you through this ancient communication technique.

Once you draw close to the vibration of the drum, your body settles and falls in line with the steady beat. Your day slows, your worries float away. There is only you and the call of Mother Earth realigning. You are grounded once again. Stay in the moment. Feel the beat. Move in and join the circle to amplify the connection.

There is a renewed understanding. Follow the natural emerging rhythms and allow your higher self to balance the body, mind and spirit. This is an alignment synchronized within the Earth vibration. Come and join me as we journey within and drum together.

Finding your drum. This will be another stopping point so that you can find a drum or percussion. You may already have one or you may choose to get one or you may want to build your own drum or percussion. You can use a box, a pot, table top or a jar with coins. Create or find someplace to create a drum sound. Please follow this very important lesson.

Important: Drumming alone is one thing. Drumming in a group is quite another! There is always a basic beat in a group. Others complement. (Martha) The rhythm in the group can easily balance your body and allow your mind and soul to just be.

Health note: If anyone is having irregularities with their heart beat than drumming a slow steady pace will help to regulate the rhythm once again.

EXERCISE III: MEDITATION

DRUMMING

Begin to drum. Close your eyes, take a deep breath, relax and drum. Move your hands back and forth, up and down and begin to rhythmically follow a pattern of personal alignment for your mind, body and soul. Continue to drum for at least ten minutes. There is no right or wrong. No judgment of self is allowed, just begin to create a steady rhythm. You can start a beat and then change it as often as you desire. Faster, slower, harder or softer. Just drum, drum and drum once more until we beat as one once again. Fall into alignment with Mother Earth, follow the pattern of your heart beat and the universal rhythm of life flow energy.

EXERCISE IV: SELF REFLECTION

What did you see?

_____
_____
_____
_____

What did you feel?

_____
_____
_____
_____
_____

What did you hear?

_____
_____
_____
_____
_____

What did you experience?

_____
_____
_____
_____
_____

Notes to self:

_____
_____
_____
_____
_____

EXERCISE V: HOMEWORK

Drumming is a wonderful way of moving yourself into a meditative state that allows the mind chatter to quiet and only allows for an artistic flow of energy to pulse through your body. It is Mother Earth calling to your soul's vibration for realignment. You generally will be invigorated as well as peaceful at the end of a drumming or rattle session. Plan to carve out a few minutes for the next several days and drum. Stop and feel the rhythm of life. Our bodies are filled with blood. Your heart has a steady rhythm and your blood pulses within your veins to follow the flow at every beat. Drumming brings you back to a basic primal existence that is engaging, enthralling and exhilarated within a unified life-force once again. Watch and see how much differently you become attuned and realigned within your life pattern.

For best results plan for one lesson at each session.

Lesson 8: A World of Water

EXERCISE I: INTRODUCTION

Have you taken the time to think about water? What is the importance of water, the feel of it, the smell of it or its properties? Water is unique two Hydrogen molecules combine with a single Oxygen molecule to create a new substance of H_2O. Trace minerals are attached which will create unique tastes. In this exercise we will be exploring water and how it affects each of us in the world today.

EXERCISE II: INFORMATION

We will explore the following topics in Your World of Water

* Human beings and our bodies of water ...

* How do the tides move you ...

* When you stand at the shore line what do you see ...

* How do you test the water ...

* The veil of water and the world beyond ...

The Miracle of Water

I have always been drawn to water. Water is where I find peace from a hectic world. According to PLOSONE over half of the world's population lives within 200 kilometers of water. Why is that? Perhaps it is that a body strives to be rebalanced by the negative ions that are omitted at the ocean or is it your skin and pores naturally open to the environment to move moisture from without to within.

Dr. Masaru Emoto, the author of *The True Power of Water* has done extensive research about water and how energy can affect its cellular structure. He studies water consciousness. The intent of positive and negative energies are focused towards water molecules. The sample is frozen to see the physical changes that have occurred. It very interesting reading and well worth the time.

Water is a clear liquid. It can be hot or cold. Let's examine some of the unique qualities of this substance. It is the only substance in the world that has three different scientific properties. Water can be a liquid, a solid as ice or become a vapor when boiled to steam. It is important to gather some basic information as we explore the world of water.

Water is the most abundant compound on Earth's surface, covering about 70 percent of the planet. In nature, water exists in liquid, solid, and gaseous states. It is in dynamic equilibrium between the liquid and gas states at standard temperature and pressure. At room temperature, it is a tasteless and odorless liquid, nearly colorless with a hint of blue. Many substances dissolve in water and it is commonly referred to as the universal solvent. Because of this, water in nature and in use is rarely pure and some of its properties may vary slightly from those of the pure substance. It is important to note that there also are many compounds that are essentially, if not completely, insoluble in water. Water is the only common substance found naturally in all three states of matter and it is essential for all life on Earth. Water usually makes up 55% to 78% of the human body.

Hippocrates, the Father of Medicine, discovered the therapeutic qualities of seawater by noticing the healing affects it had on the injured hands of fishermen. The seawater not only restricted infection risks, but patients who followed treatments involving the use of seawater found that it also promoted pain relief. It is now known that sea salt therapy is an effective treatment that assists in the rejuvenation of the cells and also induces a healthy exchange of minerals and toxins between the blood and the water. Thalassotherapy, which is the therapeutic use of the ocean, its climate, and marine products like algae, seaweed, and alluvial mud, as noted by spatrade.com are as follows:

1) Immune System. Immunity refers to the natural healing power and defense power that is inherent to living organisms. It refers to resistance against viruses and bacteria. This means the improvement in natural healing power is served.

2) Endocrine System. The endocrine system refers to the adjustment of bodily functions that are critical for sustaining life. Thalassotherapy has the potential to recover a low responsiveness of hypothalamic-adrenal endocrine system, which is caused by stress.

3) Relaxation. Studies showed that positive psychological effects were noted such as peace of mind, vibrant life, increased energy level, stability and self-control. Subject's regained self-confidence, demonstrated better introspection, and improved response behavior against stress. Improvement in the quality of sleep was indicated.

4) Metabolism. Seaweed helps to balance circulation that improves oxygenation and nutrition of the connective tissues. Thus, it can be stated that seaweed, speeds up local metabolism allowing the body's own lipolytic (fat-burning) enzymes to access fat in hard to reach places. This is characteristic of cellulite and other figure conditions where the atrophying of the connective tissue prevents proper irrigation of interstitial fluid via the Circulatory and Lymphatic Systems. Laminaria, Ascophyllum and Fucus Algae are rich in organic iodine, which stimulates metabolism.

5) Skin Allergies. Sea-bathing gives an antiseptic effect to the skin and reduces histamine in the body which causes inflammation and itching sensation. The National Pediatric Hospital, allergy section, has been giving the therapy since 1988 with many successful results. The balancing effects of seaweed on circulation leave the skin's complexion radiant with an even tone and coloring.

6) Anti-inflammation. Seaweed flushes out toxins and by-products of metabolism via the lymph system. This is valuable in the elimination of trapped fluids around the joints. White Algae, which is rich in calcium and magnesium, plays an important role in the elimination of fluids and acts as an anti-inflammatory agent.

There are many varieties of seaweed and kelp that naturally grow in the oceans. The species change based on natural elements, water temperatures, light and amount of saline within immediate area. No land plant even remotely approaches seaweeds as sources of metabolically-required minerals (Bergner 1997). Seaweeds can provide minerals often absent from freshwater and food crops grown on mineral-depleted soils. Minerals found in seaweed, noted by Sea Vegetation-envirohealthtech include: calcium, magnesium, potassium, sodium, iron, iodine, chromium and copper. As these minerals are ingested it absorbs and naturally reduces or eliminates radioactive elements and heavy metal contaminates from the body.

According to Minerals.net, the color range of Halite (salt) can be caused by impurities, the deep blue and violet colors are actually caused by defects within the crystal lattice, and the pink and peach colors of many dry Lake Halite specimens are caused by bacteria from various algae.

Astrology and the persuasion of water is significant as it affects personal characteristics. Three Astrological water signs are as follows: (ignitepoint.com)

1. CANCER (June 22-July 22)
Feelings, emotions, and deep personal conversations are what motivates and stimulates this water sign. Sensitive to a fault, Cancer is often more concerned with your feelings and needs then their own.
2. SCORPIO (October -November 21)
Scorpios can be psychic and secretive. When they can no longer withstand the emotions of the world, they often retreat into their own private worlds.
3. PISCES (February 19-March 20)
Trust is a big need of theirs, which the earth signs can bring to water. In fact, Pisces can be so emotional that the simplest things can get blown out of proportion into big dramatic scenes.

Water is most significant and highly noted as powerful within the Bible. It cleansed away old issues and renewed the soul during baptism. Holy water has been blessed and used repeatedly for healing the sick, the lame, to restore sight, to remove "dis-ease" of all types. Water was walked on, parted for safe passage and gifted from the rocks in the middle of a dessert as the life force of mankind. Throughout the Old and New Testament of the Bible, water is referenced as the healing and life sustaining substance of all man.

In Feng Shui, the water element carries the vibration for prosperity and abundance. Water character traits are creativity, wisdom, sensitivity, reflection, persuasion, effectiveness and desire for life (astrology.com/feng-shui-water)

Reflection of Water

I find myself drawn to a shoreline. Do you? The water always feels peaceful, gentle, and I notice I breathe a little deeper and relax more with every exhale. When you look at water what do you see? There are many ways to see water it is all about your frame of mind and intent in that moment.

When you stand on the shoreline, do you see the sparkling surface of sunlight along the top like diamonds dancing on the water? The intensity of light is more acute during the morning hours, as the sun welcomes a new day. Even when the water's surface is a still calm, it mirrors your surroundings. The surface of the shoreline is filled with waves ranging from tiny mounds moving forward to crashing waves pounding the shoreline. The ocean is powerful, beautiful, peaceful, or angry, within each day based on the tides, the wind, and the undercurrents. No matter the intensity, it is in constant motion with its unique rhythm of life.

Take time to slow your mind and look into the still, calm surface. Do you see the white puffy clouds, the trees along the shoreline, the brilliant sun or moonlight dancing along the surface? Perhaps you see a beautiful bird as it gently soars above your head. You see it softly floating along the glorious reflection for your eyes to behold.

Look at the water again, now what do you see? Do you see beneath? There are secrets presented lovingly within the water. There is an entire world that is vibrant and thriving under the surface. Take a moment to observe the inner dynamics. You may see fish swim by, a crab or a shell. You can see the bottom in some areas, the waving seaweeds, bright coral, other shellfish, a passing turtle or perhaps a nesting fish and watch it gently wave the tailfin to protect the next generation.

When you stand near fresh water the life rhythm is different. Are there ripples that mesmerize at a lake or pond on a calm day? Look deeply into a rain puddle see the invisible life it holds, and feel the heartbeat of Mother Earth.

Water can be babbling as it flows in a brook or stream, gathering energy as it weaves around the rocks, as it gently wears away the hardened edges of stone. Water may be powerful, loud and crashing as is experienced at Niagara Falls. The immense strength is nearly overwhelming for the mind to conceptualize. The sheer power, force and beauty all mixed together provide basic sustenance to Mother Earth. Each of our bodies and cells realign to match the magnitude of strength and power that we possess!

When you look below, what you see far below is a gorge. Thousands of years carefully wear away the edges of the rocks carving a trench deep into Mother Earth. The water starts in the north and gently flows to the south moving particles within to ramble down the stream to where it joins the sea. There are a few anomalies or southbound waters such as the Nile, the St. Johns and the Amazon Rivers. Water flows together to become one. All the earth's water is connected.

Think about your life. Are we not the same? Life and events flow in and out of our lives. Some are choices and decisions and others are circumstances that add to your lives.

These "surprise" events are already planned by God for your learning in this Earth School and recorded in the Akoshic Record. Just like a difficult assignment in school, you respond with confusion at first, then use your previous experience to build strategies to solve this problem. Thing about learning to read, or division problems. The event can easily throw your world upside down, or it may feel as if your footing has evaporated. One of the reasons that this can be so upsetting is that you truly were caught off guard by the event, and you had or still may have no control of how to solve it. This is where faith, intuition and choices do come in. We may not be able to control the circumstances, but we can always control how we choose to react and or accept the change.

Time is like a river. It will continue to pass. How you travel the river and ford the rapids is up to you. Remember, even if you choose to do nothing it too is a choice which will create its own consequences.

EXERCISE III: MEDITATION

The World of Water

Find a quiet place to sit and relax. Be certain that all phones are shut off and you will be uninterrupted for about ten minutes. Sit quietly and start to Close your eyes and begin to quiet your thoughts, breath slowly in and out. Let your body relax. Sit comfortably straight up in a chair with your palms open. Breathe in filling your lungs and keep filling until you feel it move deep within – now slowly release the breath, exhale – exhale – exhale until you are totally empty. Slowly inhale and exhale allowing your mind to just be. Adjust your body for comfort, focus your mind and your thoughts on your breath. If thoughts enter, bless and release them while you continue to breath and relax deeper with each breath.

It is a beautiful warm day you find yourself with time to be still. Imagine yourself walking and wandering along as it is time to take a journey, your journey. You have always felt at peace near water so this is where you find yourself going at this time. You have walked along your journey until you find yourself at the shoreline. It is quiet here today you look up and down the beach and don't see anyone else – just you and the beautiful surroundings all around. You see the water in front, a few seagulls in the far distance, the sun shining upon your face with a few white pillow clouds slowly dancing across the sky.

Take another deep breath and feel the peace. You hear the waves gently lapping the shoreline and the same waves of peace are now gently washing through you one breathe at a time. The water is so powerful and yet so peaceful all at one time. It is in constant motion, building to a point of total fulfillment where it must break at the top and overflow back into itself. The water it is the same water, but how differently it now looks. It has turned white and frothy and isn't the iridescent blue green of when at rest. Each wave is unique and so beautiful to observe. Feel the mist or foam, experience the fulfilling internal release of self, life and worry with every wave.

Walk to the shoreline and stand in the wade pool so that it ever so gently fills and laps over your feet. That continued peace and tranquility has now erased all jiggered rocks in your life. This moment is your moment when time has opened up this secret paradise. It is a special gift just for you. Enjoy the cool water as it glides over your toes and recedes back into the sand.

Your body feels at home, we are made of water and the water within you is calling to be home. Every cell and your soul is now blending with the sea. The flow of your blood is blended with the rhythm of the waves in which you now stand. All is one.

The water is vibrant and full of Mother Earth's knowledge. The sea is connected to lands, countries, continents thousands of miles away and is still one. Listen, listen closely to the waves that are coursing through your soul.

> What do you hear?
>
> What do you feel?
>
> What is the truth and lessons that you need to know?

Be. Be in the moment of each wave as it moves through your body filling you with eternal knowledge

> What does it say?
>
> Where are you today?
>
> What is for now?
>
> What is your most precious gift?
>
> What is your journey?

You have received the messages and now sit a moment reflecting upon this most beautiful gift of knowledge which has been graced to you.

The sun shifts and you know it is time to leave this beautiful space of existence and return to your world once again. You stand and walk away from the shoreline. Time passes more quickly as you find yourself coming back. You are back to the here and back to the now. Take a deep breath in and out, come back to this time, back to this room, back to this space and in your seat. Take another deep cleansing breath and open your eyes when you feel that you can.

EXERCISE IV: SELF REFLECTION

What did you see?

_____
_____
_____
_____

What did you feel?

_____
_____
_____
_____
_____

What did you hear?

_____
_____
_____
_____
_____

What did you experience?

_____
_____
_____
_____
_____

Notes to self:

_____
_____
_____
_____
_____
_____
_____

EXERCISE V: HOMEWORK

Take a bath. Fill the tub, feel the water, watch the water. Feel free to add bubbles or salts and experience the love that is being offered to you by the water. It would be lovely to add some gentle music and perhaps a candle. Enjoy a bath of pure luxury and spiritual connection to water. Experience the exchange of water from within to without and vice versa.

Fill a glass bowl half full with water. Stare at the water in the bowl. With your fingers gently pick up some water and let it slowly drip back into the bowl. Continue this practice several times. This is an easy way to move your mind into a meditative state. Nostradamus would stare into a bowl of water before writing his quatrains.

Take a shower. Be in the moment of the shower, and experience a cleansing process fully.

Record your experience for later reflection.

For best results plan for one lesson at each session.

Lesson 9: Tree of Life

EXERCISE I: INTRODUCTION

Your life is as unique as each tree that expresses itself on Mother Earth. We will explore the similarities of our lives with that of a tree in this lesson. Each event in nature effects a trees growth life cycle, just as each event in your life effects your growth. A tree can be made of hard or soft wood. It may easily bend and flow with the blowing wind or stay ridged to be point of breaking. Within this exercise, we will explore the similarities and differences of trees and how they relate within your world.

EXERCISE II: INFORMATION

There are over 23,000 different kinds of trees in the world (NCSU.edu). Tree wood is a highly organized arrangement of living, dying and dead cells. Trees are the largest living organism on earth. Some coastal redwoods grow to be 360 feet tall, while giant sequoia trees can weigh 2,000 tons (4 million pounds) and live for 2,500 years. One large tree can provide a days' worth of oxygen for up to four people.

The significance of a tree as a symbol of Universal Law can be found in all religions. Dendrolatry, refers to the tendency of many societies throughout history to worship or otherwise mythologize trees. Trees have played an important role in many of the world's culture and religions, as well as have been given deep and sacred meanings throughout the ages. Human beings, observing the growth and life cycle of trees, the elasticity of their branches, the sensitivity and the annual decay and revival of their foliage, see them as powerful symbols of growth, decay and resurrection. The most ancient cross-cultural symbolic representation of the universe's construction is the World Tree (Wikipedia.org).

The image of the Tree of Life is also a favorite in many mythologies. Various forms of trees also appear in folklore, culture and fiction, often relating to immortality or fertility. These often hold cultural and religious significance to the peoples for whom they appear. For them, it may also strongly be connected with the motif of the World Tree.

Other examples of trees featured in mythology are the Banyan and the Peepal (*Ficus religiosa*) trees in Hinduism, and the modern tradition of the Christmas Tree in Germanic mythology. The Tree of Knowledge of Judao-Christian, tradition as well as the Bodhi tree in Buddhism and Saglagar tree in Mongolian Tengriism. In folk religion and folklore, trees are often said to be the homes of tree spirits. Historical Druidism as well as Germanic tradition appear to have involved cultic practice in sacred groves, especially with the oak. The term "druid" itself possibly derives from the Celtic word for "oak".

Symbols of trees can be found in all cultures. The Egyptian *Book of the Dead* mentions sycamores as, "where the soul of the deceased finds blissful repose" (Wikipedia.org).

You can spend a lifetime studying the significance of trees in religion. As fascinating as it is, we will limit our discussion for this lesson.

A tree starts from a seed that had gently fallen to the ground where it made its way into Mother Earth. The rain and sun nourished the seedling until it breaks free of its shell and the tap root begins its explosion of life. It cautiously meanders through the fallen leaves into the dirt finding strength within Mother Earth. And thus, a tree is born. It is small, fragile and susceptible to the surrounding environment. With each day and with proper nourishment, the tree evolves, establishing deeper roots and becoming strong.

The seed does not resemble the tree in any way, and yet the entire greatness of the tree to come resides in the tiny seed. As the tree grows to its splendor, it is subjected to harsh elements which fashion it rings, and records its history as its magnificence is revealed.

Mother Nature changes too. Each season brings a new and different type of beauty and life. The spring is a time of new birth. The warmer weather and showers bring forth new branches stretching from larger limbs. Later, leaves will slowly emerge through the bark. This is where all the energy within has an opportunity to spring forth so that each leaf can capture the sunrays for itself. This process feeds nutrients into the tree itself, adding to the deepening of roots and strength to the limbs and often times baring fruit.

Summer is a time to celebrate and bask in the glory of where you are and what you can become. Enjoy the long days, gentle nights and warm breezes. Each day provides experiences for new growth and strength. As fall approaches the air changes and crispness nips around you. The trees signal a time of change and each leaf filled to the brim now closes as it is their time for the show. Their shapes are full, each color shines forth brilliantly portraying a multicolored canvas across mountains and valleys of the earth. Each leaf works diligently to out shine the colors of their neighbors. Greens, yellows, oranges, reds, ambers and gold are all around twisting and turning, showcasing all its brilliance with the autumn breezes. Once fulfilled they gently cover the ground below providing a patchwork carpet of warmth and protection to its very own roots to ensure a safe winter.

Winter approaches. Like the tree this is the time to slow down and work within. It is time to take all that has been learned and experienced and to reflect upon the lessons. This is the time for bark to grow a bit thicker, to rest, and preserve our resources, more reflective. You review what has transpired, evaluate and, acknowledge relevant feelings. Take time to plan as to where to go next. This time is critical in each life. How often do we rush along and not take time to stop, reflect and plan before acting? Where is your winter? How can you be your best without reviewing what can make you better?

EXERCISE III: MEDITATION

This will be a different type of meditation as you will examine a tree from your perspective. Please get paper, pencil, crayons, pens or any medium you prefer and let us create your personal tree. Take a few deep cleansing breaths. Quiet your mind and body. Relax and sit comfortably. Inhale deeply and then exhale again. Prepare your paper and writing tools. You don't have to be an artist. This is not about your artistry this is about going within yourself to learn more about your roots and basic foundation. Just participate and watch yourself grow through the process. Answer the questions and then draw your tree:

How deep are your roots and what are gives you strength?

_____
_____
_____
_____
_____

Branches are the unique experiences in your life. You travel on side paths as far as you need to, then return to your core to create another branch.

How many branches do you have?

_____
_____

What type of tree are you?

_____
_____

Describe your tree?

_____
_____
_____
_____
_____
_____
_____
_____
_____
_____

Note: our tree will evolve over time, so enjoy revisiting this experience as your heart, body and soul grows in your light.

Draw Your Tree

Your Tree of Life

Find a quiet place to sit and relax. Be certain that all phones are shut off and you will be uninterrupted for about ten minutes. Sit quietly and start to close your eyes and begin to quiet your thoughts, breath slowly in and out. Let your body relax. Sit comfortably straight up in a chair with your palms open. Breathe in filling your lungs and keep filling until you feel it move deep within – now slowly release the breath, exhale – exhale – exhale until you are totally empty. Slowly inhale and exhale allowing your mind to just be. Relax your body, your mind and your thoughts with each breath. When thoughts enter bless them and release while you continue to breath and relax deeper with each breath.

Take time to slow down and ask yourself these questions – listen within to hear the answers.

How thick is your bark? What has made you so hard?

_____
_____
_____
_____
_____

Your life has many aspects as does each tree branch – responsibilities, time commitments, friends, and family. Label your branches.

_____
_____
_____
_____
_____

Is your tree balanced? _____

What do you see happen in nature as a result of having unbalanced branches? How do you think it could be any different for you?

_____
_____
_____
_____
_____

Where does your tree grow? Are you in an open field or deep within a crowded forest?
_____
_____
_____
_____

What type of soil does your tree grow in? Are their toxins nearby?
_____
_____
_____
_____

Look around your tree base, what and who are your supports?
_____
_____
_____
_____

Name your power sources. What recharges you and provides you with strength and willpower to accomplish more?
_____
_____
_____
_____

Look at your tree – do other animals share your space, creatures that have made homes within your branches nesting and starting worlds of their own? Perhaps these creatures have burrowed through the bark and lay within? Name them.
_____
_____
_____
_____

Who lives in your tree? Parasitic or plants? Animals? Insects? Butterflies v/s termites, fungus/mushrooms?

___

Do they feed you or are they feeding off you?

___

This is such a key note please remember to periodically evaluate intentions of those in your life to ensure that it is for your best and highest good. This is YOUR life and only you can make those adjustments.

___

Your tree is covered with leaves all over the outside – what are others seeing within those leaves?

___

What do you see within each of your leaves?

___

What do you want to see within your leaves? What do you want others to see in your leaves?
_____
_____
_____
_____
_____

Do you soften in spring and leave yourself open to new opportunities of love – friendships, growth?
_____
_____
_____
_____
_____

What colors are in your tree? What colors do your leaves showcase – why?
_____
_____
_____
_____
_____

Do you grow any seeds or fruit?
_____
_____
_____
_____
_____

Perhaps you share your tree with fairies, gnomes and leprechauns. What light or magic do you see within and around you?
_____
_____
_____
_____
_____

This is YOUR tree. Examine it once again as a whole. Is it balanced? Do your branches or spirits living in your tree have the best intentions for you? If not perhaps you could sacrifice a branch to save the trunk. Spring will come and you can always grow a new branch as long as the illness doesn't continue to eat away and destroy the core of your existence.

How do you absorb the light? Where do you find light sources? Who are your light sources?

_____
_____
_____
_____
_____

Do you look up for strength, to the sun or a source of light and love? Or do you feel your strength coming from within you trunk?

_____
_____
_____
_____
_____

What nourishment do your roots receive from Mother Earth?

_____
_____
_____
_____
_____

You have recorded your life map in this tree of your life. You have been gifted with some insight as to your existence. It is time to come back. Take a few deep breaths. Return to this room, return to this seat, feel your body, your hands and your feet and open your eyes when you are ready.

Life fora is inevitable. As our bodies have evolved from infancy, each season we grow and change. We mature as the decades of our lives pass.

Our youth is captured within the spring. The lands are tilled, and seeds are planted. The sprouts emerge in vacant soils. Youth encapsulates the wonder of new, the learning about life, how it operates and experiencing all that one can without fear and worry. Spring is fresh and soft. Rains make the plants grow and everything feels alive and full of potential and promise.

Summer is the time of having families, when our careers flourish and we celebrate what is around us. We live life fully, savoring our relationship with Mother Earth. Summer is full of lushness from the elements.

The sun shines brightly and life is so very active. We are consumed by the experiences with love, children, professions and creation of self.

Fall approaches bearing fruit, brilliance of colors adjusting to the change in elements. This is a time to showcase our wisdom and life-lessons of knowledge. It is our chance to develop our relationship with God, and this blessed life that we have experienced. This is the time for ultimate growth both inside and outside, to leave your mark upon this earth! This is the time that the new seeds of life are gently released to lay dormant until spring revitalizes for new growth.

As winter approaches we become a bit slower and quieter. This is a time to reflect upon the meaning of what we have accomplished, and create documentaries of our wisdom. These are guides for others to follow so they may avoid some of the pitfalls that we encountered. We all know the best lessons in life are the ones that we experience firsthand as long as we take the time to understand the lessons which are presented. Dormancy of the outside allows for reflection and developing within. Our ascension progresses more quickly without having to repeat experiences.

When it is time to pass from this existence to the next, it is just another season. Winter may be here on this earth plane but the birth of a spring is in your next. Have you taken the time to truly understand your purpose here in this life? What have you come to accomplish? What is your personal legacy to the world? What are the lessons that you needed to learn? What will you continue to lean as you continue to breathe?

Time continues to pass along with each season. Take the time today to understand where you are on your journey. Now is the time to showcase all that you are. Go forth brilliantly and shine your light in the world. Celebrate the tree of YOU!

EXERCISE IV: SELF REFLECTION

What did you see?

_____
_____
_____
_____
_____

What did you feel?

_____
_____
_____
_____
_____

What did you hear?

___

What did you experience?

___

Notes to self:

___

EXERCISE V: HOMEWORK

Create and maintain a daily journal. The tree of life exercise is a wonderful self-evaluation tool that should be continued. A wonderful time to revisit this activity may be for New Year's or perhaps your birthday as a special gift to yourself. You will be amazed of the variety of trees that will flow through your life. New branches will sprout by your choices life will create the best growth for you.

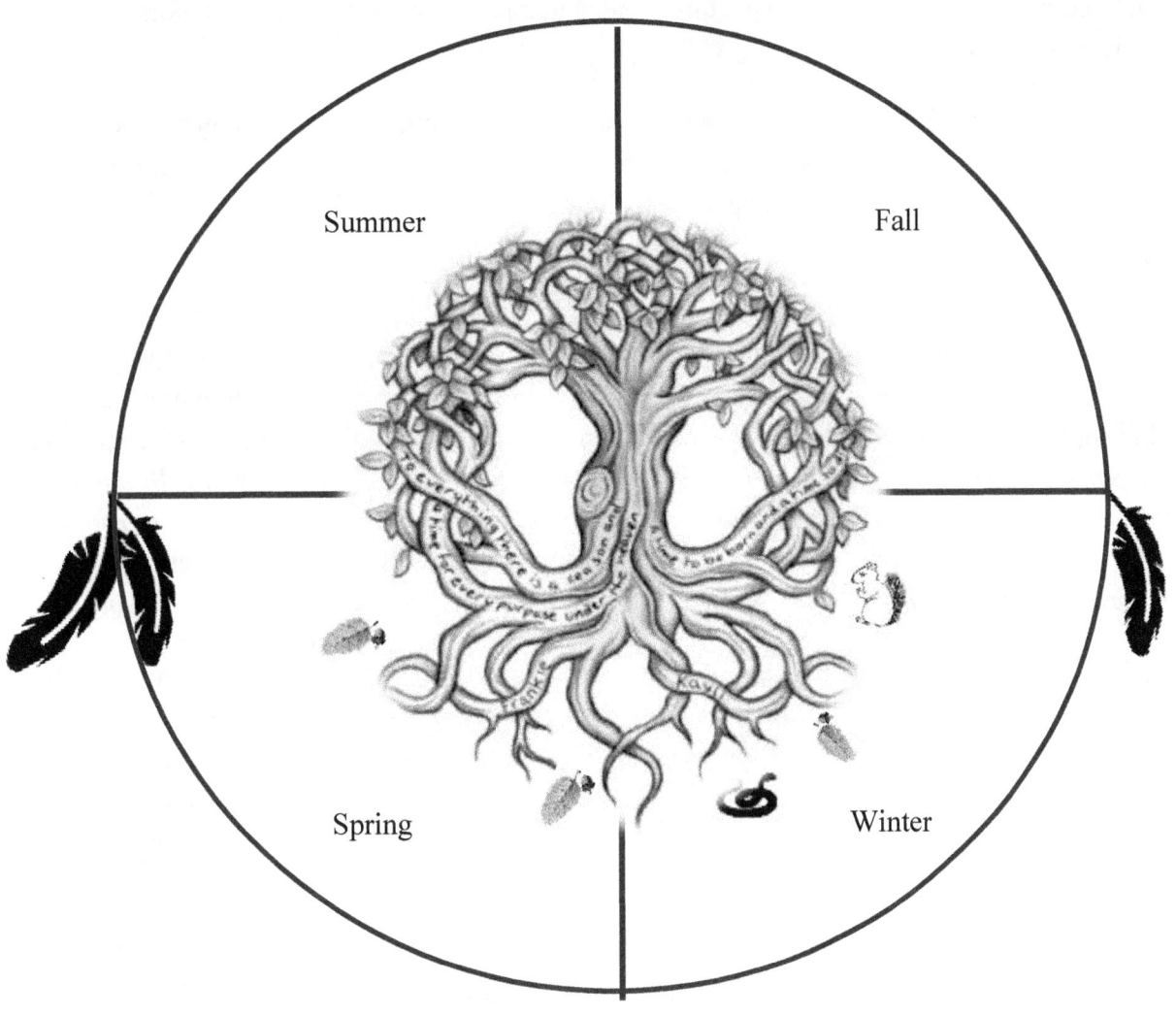

For best results plan for one lesson at each session.

Lesson 10: Dance with a Dragonfly

EXERCISE I: INTRODUCTION

Dragonflies have been around for more than 180 million years. They have beautiful jewel-like-coloring. The bright colors develop over time reflecting an idea that maturity creates the true colors within each of us. This is part of dragonfly medicine.

Dragonflies are known for fast flight and amazing aerial feats, changing directions on a dime. They twist, turn, up, down and even backwards all in an instant. They can fly up to 30 miles per hour. Life sometimes emulates these same erratic patterns of speed and flight.

EXERCISE II: INFORMATION

A dragonfly exists and thrives in both land and water; however, a metamorphosis must take place to support this amazing transformation. When a dragonfly shows up in your life, you may need fresh air in regard to something emotional. You may need to gain a new perspective. According to Steven D Farmer, *Animal Spirit Guide*, *"dragonfly can be more than a simple change, you're going through a major transformation, so enjoy the process. This is a time when magic and mystery of life is reawakening for you. You're being entirely too rational about everything and really need to tap into your deep emotions… It's important now to recharge your psychic energy, which you can do by regularly meditating"*.

Dragonfly embodies a stripping away of all the beliefs that say we can't achieve a dream or goal. It is to remind us that anything is possible when we really have true understanding. We are part of Spirit, and as such, we have the power to manifest anything that we desire. Dragonfly is the keeper of dreams, the knower within that sees all of our true potential and ability. Dragonfly strips away the illusions we are not worthy or capable when in fact it is our birthright and our true power to create anything we choose!

Dragonfly also connects us with the power of color and the ability to work with many different colors to achieve anything we want to experience in life. We can begin to see how the colors worn in clothing, the colors that decorate homes, even the color of the car driven can impact our environment for better or worse. If, for example, we continually wear dull, drab colors, while asking for more adventure or excitement-in life sends the message to the Universe that we do not really want what we are asking for. The colors with which we surround ourselves definitely sets up a vibration that attracts circumstances and energies that reflect back what messages we are sending forth. If we want change, we need to affirm that we are ready and willing for the changes to occur through the use of color vibrations that match the energy that is being sought to experience. According to Lynx Graywolf from Morningstar Nerfirm.com, if one wants to become better recognized for the work one loves doing, wearing shades of red or violet will help achieve that goal. For new beginnings try wearing shades of green. To feel more empowered try wearing shades of yellow. To feel more deeply connected with the Universe and to develop greater intuitive ability, all shades of blues and indigo are excellent! Color is a very valuable tool in expressing who we are, who we desire to be and what we desire to experience in our lives. Look at the world around you: All of nature sets forth its intent and requests through the use of a vast array of color. A flower will attract a pollinator through its color. A Tree Frog may warn predators that it is not good to eat through the colors it displays on its body. A Lion can attract a mate through the color of his mane. Dragonfly can also teach us how to use color to attract that which we desire or at least, to understand what messages we ourselves are putting forth through the colors we wear!

When Dragonfly appears, be ready for transformation! This is a long cycle that can take up to two years or more and yet the work and effort are well worth it in the end. At times you may feel like you are fire-walking your way through life. Dragonflies are really mini Dragons after all! Yet what is emerging from within you is a sense of your own inner power and faith in a Higher Power that no one can ever take from you! You are in the process of coming to know and understand who you truly are, of connecting with the vast source of power and energy that was given to you by Spirit at the time your Soul came into being. This power has grown within you as you have journeyed through space and time. Now is the time for it to be claimed as your own so you may step forth renewed as the powerful Soul that you came to this earth to express!

Dragonflies emulate the power of light, the iridescent jewel colors reflect differently dependent upon the light around and can shine more brilliantly as the light shines within and throughout.

Dragonfly Indications

- *You are being entirely too rational and need to tap into your deeper emotions.*
- *This is a time when the magic and mystery of life is awakening for you.*
- *Examine the illusions in your life.*
- *Where do you dance in life?*
- *Your transformation at this time is significant.*
- *What has dragonfly come to teach you today?*

Dance

What is Dance? According to *Webster's Dictionary*, it is to move rhythmically usually to music, using prescribed or improvised steps and gestures:
    To leap or skip about excitedly.
    To appear to flash or twinkle: eyes that danced with merriment.

Why is the art of dance so loved? Every culture in the world has some form of body movement to music. Dance provides grace, beauty and the freedom to move rhythmically with the musical vibrations being omitted. The body will naturally flow, follow a beat and move to the rhythm. Dance allows for freedom, excitement, and energy to flow through your body and into Mother Earth once again. Dance is fun, lighthearted and is non-judgmental of oneself. Young children will instinctually dance when they hear and experience music.

Watching dance can be beautiful, artistic and it is able to sweep one away into another dimension of pure grace and joy. Dance is also used in religious ceremonies because it transforms our persona and vibration. Cultural dances bond members of a tribe. It is time to move once again only now we travel within.

EXERCISE III: MEDITATION

Dance with a Dragonfly

Find a quiet place to sit and relax. Be certain that all phones are shut off and you will be uninterrupted for about ten minutes. Sit quietly and start to close your eyes and begin to quiet your thoughts. Breathe slowly in and out. Prepare your physical body. Sit up straight, but be comfortable. Sit with your arms and legs uncrossed and your palm upward on your legs. Breathe in filling your lungs and keep filling until you feel it all the way into your belly. Now slowly release the breath..., exhale – exhale – exhale, until you are totally empty. Slowly inhale and exhale, allowing your mind to just be. Relax your body, your mind and your thoughts with each breath. When thoughts enter, bless them and release while you continue to breathe and relax deeper with each breath.

It is a beautiful warm day you find yourself with time to finally relax. Imagine yourself walking and wandering along as it is time to take a journey, your journey. You have always admired the mountains, their colors, the strength, and the fresh smells of mother earth, the sweet flora that breaks through and around centuries of rocks layered upon each other building the surface of where you stand today. It is a lovely fall day the leaves have been slightly bitten by frost and have begun to metamorphose into their most glorious colors of the season. The red, yellow, orange and golden leaves are brilliant as the sun dapples though each, ever changed by a soft and steady breeze.

Let worries, concerns and thoughts just float away. You begin your assent up the mountain. There is a small worn path of pine needles, leaves and soft moss to cushion your steps as you walk up the mountain side. Your feet move softly and quietly along the path as each foot gently blends with nature. Feel the warm sun, the light breeze gently blowing against your skin as you hear the soft rustling of the whistling trees. Now take a moment to listen. The winds are Mother Earth softly trying to get your attention. You have been busy with life and not taking enough time to just be and listen to what she has to say. Great Spirit is calling for you to follow your heart.

Life is like the path that you now walk. The path wanders back and forth, around a tree or rock. A root is hidden beneath the leaves but can easily unbalance your footing. It is easier to go around the obstacles and follow the path worn by water and time. What is your path, the path that has brought you back to this time and space in life? What do you know that is needed in the world today?

Your path is ascending. You have now made it to the top, broken through the tree line and find yourself standing on the bare mountain surface. The rocks have been worn smooth by enduring centuries of existence. Harsh winds, driving rain, and decades of storms have followed the seasons of time. You are a bit tired from the walk and find yourself settling on a jutted rock that allows you the opportunity to see and experience the magnificent view below and around you. This is a time to reflect. It is your time to be in the present.

You sit in peace amazed by the enormous beauty that surrounds the tranquility of this sacred space. The sky is brilliant blue with powder puff clouds are gently floating by, the view below is indescribably brilliant as if God took all the colors on earth and artistically and perfectly blended them to create the beauty below. The air smells so fresh and untouched by others on earth. This is a space that has just been created for you to savor this moment in time. As you sit in glory of this majestic mountain you suddenly notice a dragonfly that has come to join you. You are a bit surprised to see it as there is no evidence of other wildlife on this barren rock. It softly glides effortlessly towards you and lands beside you. How odd that it has settled so close. The iridescent blue/green of its wings are slightly fluttering from the breeze and the bulging eyes are looking at you. No, the dragonfly isn't looking at you. It is looking into you and can see into your soul.

> What does it say?
>
> What is your most precious gift?
>
> What is your journey?
>
> What is your peace?

You listen to the wisdom of this magical creature sent to provide you with this precious gift of personal insight.

You have received the messages and now the dragonfly must move along. It softly catches the current of the wind and glides away. You sit a moment reflecting upon this most beautiful gift of knowledge which has graced you.

The sun shifts. You know it is time to leave this beautiful space on earth and return to your world once again. As you stand, you breathe in deeply all that is, and start down the mountain. Time passes more quickly as you find yourself returning to here, back to now.

Take a deep breath in and out, come back to this time, back to this room, back to the room and in your seat. Feel your body- wiggle your fingers and toes. Take another deep cleansing breath and open your eyes when you feel that you can.

Take a minute to acclimate yourself then begin to ask yourself the questions below.

EXERCISE IV: SELF REFLECTION

What did you see?

_____
_____
_____
_____
_____

What did you feel?

_____
_____
_____
_____
_____

What did you hear?

_____
_____
_____
_____
_____

What did you experience?

_____
_____
_____
_____
_____

Notes to self:

_____
_____
_____
_____
_____

EXERCISE V: HOMEWORK

When was the last time that you danced? Truly just danced? It is time to do so now – it doesn't matter if you are good or not. This is the time to let your body flow and follow the vibration of music. So go now find some music and dance. Let your body flow and feel the music. Please plan to spend at least 15 minutes dancing. Close your eyes, imagine the colors of a dragon fly, relax, float, sway, twirl and move. Let your body go and be one with the music!

Be experimental and practice dance to various genres of music. Try Latin, new wave, rock, Celtic, instrumentals or symphonic. Be bold and watch how your body grows and responds to the experience of basic rhythms.

Now that you have danced, do you feel exhilarated and full of life once again? Record your impressions with the different types of music.

_____
_____
_____
_____
_____
_____
_____
_____
_____
_____
_____

Journal your thoughts, feelings, memories and images. This is personal time to explore, reflect and dream possibilities into realities.

Go for a walk in a wooded area and be totally present. Feel the experience.

Additional reading you may enjoy:
Dances for Universal Peace or Dancing with a partner or others.

For best results plan for one lesson at each session.

Lesson 11: New Beginnings of Spiritual Knowledge Through Nature

EXERCISE I: INTRODUCTION

Originally, this lesson was created for the first of the year. It is applicable at any time as each and every day is entering a new beginning and an opportunity to live life differently. This lesson provides an opportunity to be inspired by the Divine, and to set a new intent for living, rather than reacting to circumstances which are presented on your life journey.

Mother Earth possesses and offers great wisdom to us throughout our lives. However, it is up to each of us to be attuned to the subtle messages and daily guidance that is being offered by being aware and present in moments and your life. Have you ever had odd experiences such as a butterfly gently glides up to you and lands on your hand, or a bird suddenly dives from nowhere right in front of you, or perhaps you look into the yard and see a deer standing in the distance staring at you? Incidents like these happen all the time and messages are tied to each experience.

EXERCISE II: POWER PIECE PROJECT

Nurture Through Nature

This is a crafting experience. Please take some time to look around your home. Have you found that you have collected natural items? Have you picked up and saved any shells, rocks, sticks, feathers, acorns, a mysterious bone, pinecones, leather, or fur pieces? Collect items you may want to work with, or take a walk and start your collection. You may still have some unused items that were collected for your Walking Stick. Find your personal sacred space. Go to the beach, the mountains, and a field, along a roadside or to your back yard. Take some time to look around at the thousands of natural gifts that are surrounding you. See what calls to you, what comes to you and bring it back for this craft project. When you begin to look closely it is amazing what you can see. Have you ever looked at an area, looked away and then back and suddenly a feather appears? They are gifts from Angels sent as tangible messages to you.

Once you have your collection of items, it is time to create. Again create that safe and spiritual environment for this project. Play some music in the background as it assists to tap into Mother Earth. I would suggest Native American if possible. Sit in stillness for a moment, setting your intent. When you are ready, it is time to begin your creation.

So many people say they can't do this project because they aren't artistic. This is not true. You are using your mind to set limits on yourself. Your heart knows no limitation, for it is where God speaks to you. We all have many gifts and talents and it is so important to continue to explore these throughout our lives. Perhaps you struggled in the past, but try once again. Remember you are now tapping into Mother Earth, Her power, guidance and her gift to you which is to be created at this time.

You can use leather strands or twine to tie the items together, sew items or use glue. There is no right or wrong way as this is your instinctual craft. It truly is amazing at the end of this session how much natural energy you can feel from your newly created Power Piece.

Start with a base. It may be a stick, a rock or piece of wood – whatever, but it must be a natural item. Look at the piece, touch it and then tap into its energy, feel what else should be added. You can add sticks, rocks, stones, leaves, pinecones, bark, shells, feathers, fur, bones, leather or whatever you have collected. Feel free to alter the pieces. Carve the wood, add holes so that stones can be imbedded, cut the leather into various shapes or drill holes so that items can be easily attached.

You may find that you need to create several pieces. Relax and take your time. This is a gift, a special time to share the power of Mother Earth. You may find that you need to add other items later. That is fine. You will know what needs to be on your power piece.

This crafting should take at least a couple of hours. Plan to use a full table so that you can spread out all the items and feel where they fit. Don't get frustrated. Just stop and ask your Angels, Spirit Guides, God the Great Spirit, any and all celestial beings to come forth and assist in creating this magical personal piece. Pick up an item, hold it. Feel the natural power and decide where it should be placed. The best way to compete this project is to lay out all your items so that you can easily see them, have an open mind, listen within to Spirit and follow the inner guidance. It is fine to stop, take a break and then come back to add more. Look at the table of items and your creation. You may get new ideas. Enjoy your visit with nature and this crafting process!

When complete, sit and hold your creation. Bond with the energies within your new power piece. Continue to hold your piece as you enter into the meditation below.

EXERCISE III: MEDITATION

SPIRITUAL KNOWLEDGE

Find a quiet place to sit and relax. Be certain that all phones are shut off and you will be uninterrupted for about ten minutes. Sit comfortably and start to close your eyes and begin to quiet your thoughts, breath slowly in and out. Sit up straight. Be content, and sit with the palms of your hand up in your lap. Breathe in filling your lungs and keep filling them until you feel it all the way into your belly. Now slowly release the breath, exhale – exhale – exhale, until your lungs are totally empty. Slowly inhale and exhale allowing your mind to silence or be calm. Relax your body. Relax your mind and relax your thoughts with each breath. When busy thoughts enter bless and release them while you continue to breathe and relax deeper with each breath, focusing on your breath.

It is a beautiful warm day and you find yourself with time to finally relax. You wander along outside walking until you find yourself beside a stream. There is a lovely water-worn flat rock right along the edge. Sit down in a nice comfortable position and just breathe. Life has been busy, but this is your time to just sit and let the layers of life peel away one at a time with every breath that you take, slip into the water to be carried away.

Let the worries, concerns and thoughts just float away and travel down the babbling brook. Feel the warm sun. There is a light breeze gently blowing against your skin. You hear the soft rustling of the whispering trees. Now take a moment to sense all that is in the moment. The winds are Mother Earth softly trying to get your attention. You have spent the last year running through life and not taking enough time to just be and listen to what she has to say. Has it been only this year or many others? This is a time to begin the year of new. Mother Earth calls out to you this day, the very first day, with the birth of a life that has an earthen focus. Great Spirit is calling you to be and to follow your Spiritual calling in life.

Be still. Just sit and listen – to the rippling water, the whispering winds, the cries of the birds, the chatter of squirrels and the chirping of the crickets. You feel your heart beating slowly in your chest and the sound brings you back to your original roots. It is the beating of the drums, the beating of your soul. It is a slow and steady rhythm, the sound of life pulsing through your veins one beat at a time. The steady drum replicates the ticking of the greatest time clock of the Cosmos. Unite with this beat. Become this slow and steady rhythm. Listen to your spirit calling.

Heavenly Father, Great Spirit, Mother Earth, Angels and Spirit Guides, come to me now as I reflect upon my life: *

Why did I come back to this earth plain? _____

What do I need to know? _____

What is my heart calling out for? _____

What do I need to feel? _____

What must I experience? _____

What is my purpose in this life? _____

What do I need to learn to move forward? _____

Who is my Spirit Guide? _____

What is my power animal? _____

What has it come to tell me? _____

Where do I find peace and guidance from Great Spirit? _____

Where do I see myself along this life journey today? _____

This is a new beginning of your life. Take a moment to reflect upon the answers that have been gifted to you.

Did you see a person? _____

Did you hear a name? _____

What is your desire? _____

Take note as we will write them down shortly. Thank you, Father God, Great Spirit, Mother Earth, Angels and Spirit Guides for the gift of your time and guidance.

It is time to head back with the great spiritual knowledge that has been gifted to you along this journey. Take a breath in and out. Hear the stream, feel the solid rock beneath you, take a moment to be in this space. Take another deep breath and feel yourself returning to your seat in this room and time here today. Slowly open your eyes when you feel ready.

EXERCISE IV: SELF REFLECTION

Take time to acclimate back to where you are – stay in the peace as you begin to reflect.

What did you see?

_____
_____
_____
_____
_____

What did you feel?

_____
_____
_____
_____
_____

What did you hear?

_____
_____
_____
_____
_____

What did you experience?

_____
_____
_____
_____
_____

What items on your power piece hold special messages for you?

_____
_____
_____
_____
_____

This is a critical lesson. Nature speaks to us all the time, this is a primary source of information; however, we are so distracted by the life on earth plane and self-focused that we miss special messages from the higher side of life. When you moved through this meditation you were asked about animals. We all have animal spirits that are assigned to each of us. Have you ever noticed a particular animal who you frequently encounter? If you think about it you will probably know what your animal is. Take some time and research that animal. Look for animal totems and learn more about your animal and what they are saying to you. The next time you see this animal, stop and ask it for your message.

Note: Even though you may have an animal totem, other animals come to you with messages, so pay attention to animal encounters and listen for what they may be. When an animal takes the time to come to you they bring enlightening messages from beyond. Take the time to listen and hear what they gift to you.

Notes to self:

_____
_____
_____
_____
_____

EXERCISE V: Homework

Please go back and review the questions within the meditation and take notes again of your experiences. You are building a tapestry, collecting information in bits and pieces that will be lovingly woven into the pattern of your life. Take the time needed to identify, learn and listen to the information that is being gifted within each chapter of this book.

Your project may change from time to time. Feel free to add items as you are inspired by Spirit.

When an animal crosses your path take a minute to recognize this. Reflect upon the animal. Feel its Spirit to hear if there is a specific message for you.

Listen to nature. Place your palm upon a tree. Feel the pulse of life that flows deep within. Listen with your heart.

You may also feel guided and directed to create another piece for yourself or power pieces to be gifted to loved ones.

For best results plan for one lesson at each session.

Lesson 12: Fall-o-wing the Whispering Wings

EXERCISE I: INTRODUCTION

Fall is a colorful time of year. Color is filled with energy that changes as does the light that reflects each color being seen. Color holds a high vibration that reminds us to explore other high vibrational entities such as Angels and Spirit Guides. Join me as we connect to their knowledge and guidance and receive direction in our lives.

EXERCISE II: INFORMATION

This lesson celebrates the fall season, a time when the days become shorter the nights cooler. There is crispness in the air. If you live in the North or have ever visited, you can understand the majestic colors that celebrate this time of the year. The trees vary from maple, oak, birch and so many others are all moving through this transformational time. As this time of preparation and celebration meld together, each leaf is destined to change. The cold weather signals each tree to stop providing the necessary nourishment to each leaf, gifting them with an opportunity to showcase their cycle's existence. Each leaf on every tree is competing to be the most brilliant of all. The colors of red, yellow, gold and orange are highlighted against the green and brown canvas. Each leaf will quietly release itself through this transformation and blanket the earth with its brilliance.

Fall is a time of harvest. The plants and trees have grown all season and created a bounty of foods for a forest of animals. The squirrels and chipmunks scurry about gathering and storing fresh nuts. Birds collect leaves, sticks and berries to fortify their nests. Bears feast on nuts and berries preparing for hibernation. Harvest is a time of much color and great abundance for Mother Earth and Her creatures to prepare for the forthcoming winter season.

All major world religions affirm angelic beings. When thinking of Angels and Spirit Guides, brilliant colors are often experienced. Therefore, it seemed natural to blend the two together through this lesson. There is a great amount of information to absorb. You may have some experience or knowledge of this subject; however, I believe it is important to provide reminders and basic information about each of these guiding lights of the universe. Topics being discussed are: Angels, Archangels, Guardian Angels, Ascended Masters, Spirit Guides, Animal Guides and other energy beings that surround you and wish only the best for you here on earth.

According to the *Webster Dictionary*, the definition of the word "Archangel" is a high ranking Angel. They are considered to be the "leader" of the Angels. Seven Archangels appeared before God in The Book of Revelations. Only four were named in the Bible. Some of the information below will not be only from Christian faith; it will come from others that believe in the almighty as well. They are the divine messengers between humans and God.

Doreen Virtue has dedicated her life to the study of Angels and much of the information within this lesson is attributed to her work. The following angels are the most significant in the Judeo Christian heritage.

Angels:

Uriel *"God is light", "God's light", Fire of God"*

Uriel is considered one of the wisest Archangels because of his intellectual information, practical solutions and creative insight, but he is very subtle. You may not even realize he has answered your prayer until you've suddenly come up with a brilliant new idea.

Raphael *"Healing power of God", "The Divine has healed", "God heals"*

Hebrew word rapha means "doctor" or "healer". Raphael is a powerful healer and assists with all forms of healing - humans and animals. He helps to rapidly heal body, mind and spirit if called upon, as in the biblical story of Abraham and the pain he felt after being circumcised as an adult. You may call upon Raphael on behalf of someone else, but he cannot interfere with that person's free will. If they resist spiritual treatment, it cannot be forced.

Michael *"Who is like God", "Like unto God", "Who is like the Divine"*

As the first Angel created by God, Michael is the leader of all the Archangels and is in charge of protection, courage, strength, truth and integrity. Michael protects us physically, emotionally and psychically. He also oversees the light worker's life purpose. His chief function is to rid the earth and its inhabitants of the toxins associated with fear. Michael carries a flaming sword that he uses to cut through etheric cords and protects us from any lower energies. When he's around, you may see sparkles or flashes of bright blue or purple light. Call on Michael if you find yourself under psychic attack or if you feel you lack commitment, motivation and dedication to your beliefs, courage, direction, energy, vitality, self-esteem or worthiness. Michael helps us to realize our life's purpose, and he's invaluable to light workers helping with protection, space clearing and spiritual deliverance.

Gabriel *"Strength of God"; "The Divine is my strength"; "God is my strength"*

The only Archangel depicted as female in art and literature, Gabriel is known as the "messenger" Angel and is one of the four Archangels named in Hebrew tradition and is considered one of the two highest-ranking Angels in Judeo-Christian and Islamic religious lore. Apart from Michael, Gabriel is the only Angel mentioned by name in the Old Testament. Gabriel is a powerful and strong Archangel. Those who call upon her will find themselves pushed into action that leads to beneficial results.

Raguel - Ruhiel, Ruagel, Ruahel: *"Everything is how it needs to be right now. Look past the illusion, and see underlying order."*

Call on Raguel to heal arguments or misunderstanding, bringing harmony to situations, or attracting wonderful new friends. Raguel is considered to be the archangel of orderliness, fairness and justice. He also manages the relationships between angels and humans.

Ariel - Sariel, Metatron, Prosperity *"Your material needs are provided as you follow your intuition and manifest your dreams into reality."*

Archangel Ariel is believed to be a leader of the Virtues choir of angels, who govern the order of the physical universe. He watches over the sun, moon, stars, and all the planets, including Earth. Ariel is intimately involved in environmentalism.

Jeremiel- Remiel, Jerahmeel: *"Everything is happening exactly as it is supposed to, with hidden blessings you will soon understand."*

Archangel Jeremiel's specialty is developing an understanding of spiritual visions and clairvoyance. Call on Jeremiel to conduct a life review, so you can make appropriate adjustments with respect to how you wish to live. Jemiel is known as the Angel of hope; intuitive guide; greets us and escorts to heaven.

The Nine Choirs of Angels

(Doreen Virtue – spiritualconnectedness.com) Angelology, the study of angels, holds that there are nine "choirs" or branches of angels, which include the following groups:

• **Seraphim.** These are the highest order of angels, said to be shining bright, as they are closest to God. They are pure light.

• **Cherubim.** Usually portrayed as chubby children with wings such as Cupid, the Cherubim are the second-highest order. They are pure love.

• **Thrones.** The triad of Seraphim, Cherubim, and Thrones resides in the highest realms of Heaven. Thrones are the bridge between the material and the spiritual, and represent God's fairness and justice.

• **Dominions.** The Dominions are the highest in the next triad level of angels. They are the overseers or managers of angels, according to God's will.

• **Virtues.** These angels govern the order of the physical universe, watching over the sun, moon, stars, and all of the planets, including Earth.

• **Powers.** As their name implies, this choir comprises peaceful warriors who purify the universe from lower energies.

• **Principalities.** The third triad are the angels closest to Earth. The Principalities watch over the planet, including nations and cities, to ensure God's will of peace on Earth.

• **Archangels.** These are the overseers of humankind and the guardian angels. Each archangel has a specialty representing an aspect of God.

• **Guardian angels.** You, and every individual, have personal guardian angels assigned to you throughout your life.

Guardian Angels:

Guardian Angels are very significant to human beings because they are the only spirits who are intimately connected to us from the beginning of our lives to the very last breath. They watch over, guide, and nurture us-keeping our minds, bodies and souls safe until we are ready to return to spirit – and they personally walk us back to heaven.

The Angels that walk with us and around us are here to provide knowledge, guidance, support and comfort. Please understand that we need to ASK for them to enter into our lives and assist. Be open and ask for their guidance. You can call on each individually to target a specific request or just ask for the loving Angels to come and gift you at the time of your calling.

Benevolent Guides:

Spirit Guide. A spirit guide or Guardian Angel is present simply to assist you, not as an entity that controls your every move. If a spirit guide has a negative influence on your behavior, then chances are good that it's not a spirit guide at all, but something else entirely according to Patty Wigington, (pagan.wiccan.about.com). These are some of the more commonly found types of spirit guides:

Ascended Masters. These are guides often found by people who do energy work, such as Reiki. An Ascended Master who appears as a spirit guide often incarnated into a physical life and moved on to a higher spiritual plane -- for example, Buddha, Krishna, even Jesus. Ascended Masters usually work with collective groups of souls. If you've got an Ascended Master hanging around you, you're not the only one he or she is helping. Their primary focus is that of helping all of humanity. It's not uncommon for an ascended master to have access to Akashic records. Also referred to as Master Teacher guides.

Ancestral Guides. An ancestral guide is one who can claim some sort of kinship with you, such as your dear Aunt Katie who died when you were ten. They may also appear in the form of a long-dead ancestor. In some schools of thought, these entities are seen as reincarnated, because they are the spirits of someone who loved us during their physical lifetime, or who had some sort of blood connection to our family. Some people, depending on their religious upbringing, believe these types of guides as guardian angels.

Common Spirit Guide or Teacher Guide. A typical spirit guide is archetypical, symbolic or representative of something else. For example, you may find your guide appears in the form of a warrior, a storyteller, or a wise woman and they have appeared to you for a purpose. Typically, that purpose is to teach you and guide you along a particular path. They may also introduce you to other archetypes along your journey, and help out with problem solving, based upon your needs. They are known to provide insight by way of dreams or meditation, and may only remain with you as long as you need them, then move on.

Animal Guides. Although many people say they have animals as spirit guides, often these entities are more companions than anything else. It's not uncommon for a deceased pet to linger around, keeping you company through the grieving process. In some spiritual traditions, such as various Native American or shamanic paths, a person may have an animal totem, which provides teaching and protection.

My personal experience and belief is that each person has one or two primary animals that are attached to them. These animals are there to provide information and guidance throughout life. It also is important to pay attention to other animals that travel through your daily life. At various times in your life your primary animal may change based on the lessons that you have learned and the timing for personal growth.

It is just as important to pay attention to the daily animal experiences that you encounter. Get yourself an animal guide book or reference information on-line that describes animal totems. Animals will come to you and may signal you to activities, dangers, prepare you for encounters and provide you with instinctual knowledge to assist in guiding you within this life. Pay close attention to the animals that seem to speak to you. The bird that stops and stares at you, a dragonfly that mysteriously shows up in your home, a turtle that is sitting on your front step when you arrive home, a group of frogs that oddly make loud croaking noises only when you pass by and become quiet after you pass. Look around a bit more closely, be aware of your surroundings and pay attention to the animals that seem to be a constant in your life and others that pass through. If an animal is speaking to you take time to research the animal totem and then listen with your heart, you will be able to get a basic understanding of what is being said and the direction that they are leading you.

Another thing that I have found to be true is that you may need to track your visiting animals and that they may have specific individual meanings just for you. Don't place an ultimate answer from a book, but the voices and guidance from within. Follow your heart and your Spirit will open your understanding if the intended messages.

Seven Spirits of God:

As we are explore Angels, Spirits and Guides, the Bible is the traditional book to which most Christian populations relate. Therefore, I believe it is important to include the Seven Spirits of God as noted within Revelation 4 of the *Bible* from Biblegateway.com to our study:

- **The Spirit of Wisdom.** Is the quality or state of being wise; knowledge of what is true or right coupled with objective judgment as to action; sagacity, discernment, or insight.
- **The Spirit of Understanding.** Is knowledge of or familiarity with a particular thing and skill in dealing with or handling something.
- **The Spirit of Counsel.** Is an assembly of persons summoned or convened for consultation, deliberation, or advice.
- **The Spirit of Power.** Is a marked ability to do or act with strength or might; force.
- **The Spirit of Knowledge.** Is acquaintance with facts, truths, or principles, from study or investigation.
- **The Spirit of Righteousness.** Is acting in an ethical, moral way.
- **The Spirit of Divine Awfulness.** Is of pertaining to a Supreme Being, inspiring awe.

In life there are so many benevolent entities that fall within the Spirit realm. Angels are spirits without physical bodies, who possess superior intelligence, gigantic strength, and surpassing holiness. They enjoy an intimate relationship with God as His special adopted children, contemplating, loving, and praising

Him in heaven. They are bodiless entities that perform certain tasks for God and are commonly thought of as the messengers of God. Angels are good spirits, unlike their counterparts, the demons. They are usually portrayed as having a human form, being dressed in long, white clothes, surrounded by a bright light and with long, swanlike wings. They were portrayed thus by artist, often on church command, to alert the faithful that angels are more than human. There are cases, however, where angels appeared as ordinary men and were mistaken as such.

Who are our Guardian Angels? According to the *Bible*, "No evil shall befall you, nor shall affliction come near your tent, for to His Angels God has given command about you, that they guard you in all your ways" Psalm 91:10-12. He has charged His angels with the ministry of watching and safeguarding every one of His creatures that behold not His face. Kingdoms have their angels assigned to them, and men have their angels.

The light beings of love are created as extensions of God's love to be with and support mankind with our lives here on the earth plane. When you work with light, healing light and feeling the love light it is important to have some basic information of the various types of benevolent beings who may be guiding, supporting and assisting you in your life.

Below is a chart that depicts the various Angels and corresponding related information. The colors and days of the week are related to the corresponding Angels and chakras as noted from Doreen Virtue.

The Rays of the Archangels

Archangel Michael	1st Ray	Blue	Tuesday	Throat Chakra
Archangel Jophiel	2nd Ray	Yellow	Sunday	Crown Chakra
Archangel Chamuel	3rd Ray	Pink	Monday	Heart Chakra
Archangel Gabriel	4th Ray	White	Friday	Base of the Spine
Archangel Raphael	5th Ray	Green	Wednesday	Third Eye
Archangel Uriel	6th Ray	Purple & Gold flecked w/Ruby	Thursday	Solar Plexus
Archangel Zadkiel	7th Ray	Violet	Saturday	Seat of the Soul

You have spent some time reading about various Angels and Guides that are a part of your life. Perhaps you have been able to see the correlation of their presence within your world. The Angels that move through do so as requested or on an as needed basis. Angels and Spirit Guides are always around and very willing to help, however it is very important to ask for their assistance and then please don't forget to thank them for their assistance and guidance. Their presence is of great value and deserving of our gratitude.

EXERCISE III: MEDITATION

ANGELIC GUIDANCE

Find a quiet place to sit and relax. Be certain that all phones are shut off and you will be uninterrupted for about ten minutes. Sit quietly and start to Sit in a comfortable position and relax, breathe in and out. Take deep cleansing breathes, in and out, inhale slowly and exhale. Let your body relax within the chair that you are sitting. Let your body become completely relaxed, your feet, ankles, calves, thighs, buttock sand the core of your body. With each breathe you release the stresses of the day and the activities within your life. Now relax your chest, your arms through your hands, each finger, your neck and all the muscles within your face up to the crown of your head. Your body is completely relaxed.

Imagine a beautiful bubble floating in the air, you see the iridescence of the bubble as it gently floats and moves through the air. You watch the bubble as it begins to grow larger and larger and moves closer towards you. The bubble is now so large it encompasses you. Look closely within the bubble and see and feel the amazing love that is within this beautiful glowing orb. It gently invites you to enter within its sphere. As you enter, you are overwhelmed with the love that now is circling around the outside and within every cell of your being. The love is energizing, forgiving, accepting, compassionate, hopeful, showing new promise of new beginnings. Be still and let the love flow within and around your entire being. Be in the moment of this ultimate love from God and his blessed Angels.

You now look more closely and see the beautiful iridescence of love that flows around the edges are actually God's beautiful Angels. They gracefully float in and around one another to create this beautiful sphere of warm unconditional love. As you bask in this moment in time your body is lighter and you feel the reflective warmth. Look around to see each of their faces. The elegance of their body language reveals acceptance and love. Each is there just for you. See their colors. Take a moment to truly see and listen within to each ascended Spirit. There are specific messages for you. Listen carefully not with your ears but with your soul to what is being gifted to you. Take the messages and carefully place them into your memory bag so that you can easily recall their gifts. Be within this total essence of love and personal messaging. Please remember to thank them each after their message and all for the gift of love that is so graciously shared throughout your entire being.

You have now received all your messages and understand that it is time to release yourself from the bubble. It is slowly shrinking and moves outside of you once again growing smaller by the minute as it floats away. The air feels cool against your skin. Your soul is completely at peace with the love that is still vibrating within your soul. You are returning now, floating into your chair, into the room once again and into your body comfortably seated in this time and space. Take one deep cleansing breath.

Wiggle your fingers and toes and open your eyes when you feel ready. Welcome home once again. Take a few minutes to write down what you experienced. Remember you have brought back your memory bag which is specifically filled with messages from each of the Angels.

EXERCISE IV: SELF REFLECTION

You may have had experience with several of the Angels mentioned in this section. Take a few minutes to specifically write down which Angel that you believed it to be and what the delivered message was. You can always come back and fill in additional information as it is remembered.

What did you see?
_____
_____
_____
_____
_____

What did you feel?
_____
_____
_____
_____
_____

What did you hear?
_____
_____
_____
_____
_____

What did you smell?
_____
_____
_____
_____
_____

What is in your heart?
_____
_____
_____
_____
_____

Notes to self:
_____
_____
_____
_____
_____
_____

EXERCISE V: HOMEWORK

Do a bit of research on Angels. Go to one of Doreen Virtues websites, a book or work with her various Angel Cards. Her works are amazing and will be extremely inspirational.

Be sure to look up the specific Angels so that you can get a good visual of what they look like.

For best results plan for one lesson at each session.

ADDENDUM

Writing this book has been an amazing personal journey. It has truly opened into a new world for me and my loved ones. I have heard and followed the guidance that was provided. Much time was spent in prayer and meditation, opening my heart for messages from Spirit. I now share an amazing experience that transpired while writing this book.

I had just spent a few days away, relaxing and reflecting. We were on a plane headed home when I looked out the window and saw a cloud that truly resembled an Eagle. It was so clear and powerful I started to write what I saw and this is what came through. I have never channeled Angels before, but on this day and time these were clear messages. With all humility and gratitude I gift them to you, dear reader. May you be as inspired and blessed by them as I have ben by them.

Eagle Clouds

Go forth, my child, and share my story. Look within to see the world through new pure eyes. Eyes not clouded by power, greed and chaos, but eyes of faith, peace, harmony, strength, grace and love. Love of self-first, and then love of mankind. I walk with you this day and say stand strong! Let me sweep you back into your roots and connections to Mother Earth and Father God who are within.

I look at you and see all potential ready to fly! Let me carry your silly fear. I am so much greater than all. Just listen to me and share my message with the world. People have moved too far away from their natural roots. I come to you to help bridge the gap and assist in making this connection once again. My world is so precious, beautiful and such a gift to all. But, now people are just too busy and electronic that they forget to tap in and refill from my natural gift of life and energy.

See the rock or a mountain. It took centuries to create. Man comes along to tear it down or dig it up. Help Mother Earth. Share words. Your prayers and energy heal. Sit in the rain and feel the gift of water as it trickles into your being and fills you with true life.

My sun blesses light to all as my daughter. The moon shows wonder and mystery, along with romance to the world.

With each of the following messages I clearly heard the name and then the message followed. They wanted me to know who was providing the guidance. Each Angel had a different voice tone and I could feel their energies change as they each hold a unique vibration frequency.

Arch Angel Michael

I am your guide. I have much to share. Please take time to share my words and lessons. Follow my path, I have waited centuries to come back. I need your body, your writing, your eyes, your energy, but mostly your commitment to provide knowledge, love and lessons to my people.

Thank you for your service. I will always provide what you need and keep you healthy and able to fulfill our destiny. We will camp as in old, teepee style along a river. People must touch back to the sacred life to hear and learn the lessons.

Come my child, trust that I will not fail you. I will carry you through. Be pure light in life!

Arch Angel Raphael

I come to heal, and to provide strength to mankind. You must understand God has plans far beyond any Angel and some illnesses and trials must happen so you may learn your lessons in life. How can one share if they have no knowledge? I fill you with strength and pass forth Grace. I remove anger and frustration as they block and clog your gifts.

Thank you for listening. I will come again.

Ariel

I am shy and a bit quieter. I bring clouds, joy, peace and the colors in a rainbow. You are to dream. Follow the colors of joy and happiness. Share my blessings with my Earth Children.

Thank you gracious one.

Azrael

I bring strength, courage, passion to move forward and try new. I am with you and all others. You must be open to hear and invite me in. I bring unexplained power and courage. You are able to lift a car alone. It is I with you!

I am with you my child. It is time to go forward. My wings wrap around you and shelter you from outside harm. I move before you with a sword and a shield.

Be well, my child. Together we travel forward to conquer evil and over shadow, all with love.

Zadkiel

I bring kindness to the world. Take time to share and take turns. Extend words of encouragement. A smile can change a life. I look into others eyes and provide hope once again. Be my eyes! Share the gift of kindness with my children.

Be well, my child.

Chamuel

Thank you for listening. I bring charm, peace and posture. Your outside can glow as within. You are a being of light and love. Let it shine through for others to see. I love sparkles and colors! Let the brilliance of you shine brightly for the world to see.

Love, light and laughter be with you my child.

Uriel

I bring allowance to be real in life. To see, feel and experience all the world has to offer. Feel – experience – be BOLD in life! I am here to share and celebrate your feelings.

I will elevate your accomplishments and spread your word around. You are not alone. I am your messenger. Gift me with mail. Share our words with the world, my child.

Blessings to you.

These personal messages are examples of messages that you can receive too. Angels are around us at all times. Angels speak into our minds through our hearts. Angels are filled with love and great knowledge. The love that they share is a never ending bounty of pure abundance. Take a few minutes and call in your Angels. You now know how to do this. Quiet your mind, and body. Move into a relaxed and meditative state. Be still. Take deep breaths. BE! Be present. Be in the moment. Be observant. Be still. Hear their words with your hear.

Our Angels wait for your invitation.

_____
_____
_____
_____
_____

Ask the Angels for peace.
_____
_____
_____
_____

Ask the Angels for grace.
_____
_____
_____
_____

Ask the Angels for comfort.
_____
_____
_____
_____

Ask the Angels for enlightenment.
_____
_____
_____
_____

Ask the Angels for a special message.
_____
_____
_____
_____

COMING FULL CIRCLE PERSONAL ANALYSIS

Review and Reflection

Most books are read for content or entertainment. Usually after one reading, you receive the information or enjoy the experience. You may choose to share the volume with a friend, or on a rare occasion, reread a favorite section.

This book is different. It is meant to reflect your soul growth. It is your personal work book - - interactive and timeless. If you have followed the lessons and taken the time to explore yourself, you should have a better understanding of the Spiritual world and yourself. Within spiritual development there is always growth and it is ever changing. As you review the content over time and repeat the exercises, you will be amazed by the new reflections from Spirit. Continue to record your growth and be amazed!

Please take the time now to review each of the sections and your answers. Review them within the sections that they are written and take some time to reflect on your writings, guidance and enhanced insight.

The Practice of Spirituality & Healing Energy

Lesson 1 – Listening to Life

Lesson 2 – Energy Healing

Lesson 3 – The Fruits of the Spirit & Chakra's

What did you learn new about Spirituality?

_____
_____
_____
_____
_____
_____
_____

What would you like to explore further for personal development?

_____
_____
_____
_____
_____
_____
_____

What patterns did you see about yourself?

_____
_____
_____
_____
_____
_____
_____

What did you discover new about yourself?

_____
_____
_____
_____
_____
_____
_____

What special gifts did you receive from these lessons?

What you would like to incorporate into your daily life?

What is your action plan?

Notes to self:

Personal Development Through Self Exploration

Lesson 4 – Carrying the Weight of the World on Your Hips

Lesson 5 – The Spirit of Love

Lesson 6 – A True Warrior in Today's World

What did you learn new about Spirituality?

___

What would you like to explore further for personal development?

___

What patterns did you see about yourself?

___

What did you discover about yourself?

___

What special gifts did you receive from these lessons?

_____
_____
_____
_____
_____
_____

What do you want to incorporate into your daily life?

_____
_____
_____
_____
_____
_____

What is your action plan?

_____
_____
_____
_____
_____
_____

Notes to self:

_____
_____
_____
_____

Connecting with Mother Earth to Build Your Spirituality

Lesson 7 – Drumming

Lesson 8 – A World of Water

Lesson 9 – The Tree of Life

Lesson 10 – Dance with a Dragonfly

Lesson 11 – A New Year of Spiritual Knowledge through Nature

Lesson 12 – Fall-o-wing the Whispering Wing

What did you learn new about Spirituality?

_____
_____
_____
_____
_____
_____
_____
_____

What would you like to explore further for personal development?

_____
_____
_____
_____
_____
_____
_____
_____

What patterns did you see about yourself?

_____
_____
_____
_____
_____
_____
_____
_____

What did you discover about yourself?

_____
_____
_____
_____
_____
_____
_____

What special gifts did you receive from these lessons?

_____
_____
_____
_____
_____
_____
_____

What you would like to incorporate into your daily life?

_____
_____
_____
_____
_____
_____
_____

What is your action plan?

_____
_____
_____
_____
_____
_____
_____

Notes to self:

_____
_____
_____
_____
_____
_____
_____

Review and Reflection Exercise

You have spent a great deal of time, energy and intention moving beyond your known and exploring deeper within yourself to find amazing gifts and lessons within your heart. This book is not intended to be read in image fashion. This is an opening to a new doorway in your life. It is up to each of you to stand before the door, to reach out and turn the handle, to open the door, and to walk through!

Intent Declaration:
Get a red piece of paper and write.

Holy Divine Universe, (God) my heart is open and ready to receive.

_____
_____
_____
_____
_____
_____
_____
_____

Throughout the book, you have learned many lessons. You have collected spiritual items, you have created power pieces, received spiritual messages and you have found that power and energy within natural items all around us. It is a beautiful gift to self to create a sacred space in your home where items and messages can be gathered and displayed. This space can be a shelf, an end table, perhaps a windowsill or maybe you have a corner that can be dedicated as your Sacred Space. Find a special box where you can safely store your spiritual messages. It is wonderful to have your items displayed in a sacred area. Having a chair nearby makes it a perfect place to journal. Once dedicated, the space will continue to enhance your energies and spiritual journey.

Journaling is another core principle that unlocks messages from beyond to yourself. You have been practicing this exercise throughout the book. Please continue to do so and watch what you will discover. I always find it best to journal very early in the morning when the night's activities are settling down and just before the day has awakened. It seems that this is the time of great strength and wisdom which is easily shared to the seekers. Just sit in the quiet and begin to write. Do not think about what you are writing. Ask for guidance and allow the words to flow to and through you. Be sure to go back later and reread what was written as you will often be amazed by the words that are gifted through the Divine Grace of God.

INSPIRATIONAL MESSAGES

Words of Wisdom from your Loving Father

This morning I awoke and God our Father had many words to share with me. I thoughtfully walked to the shore as a bird kept diligently calling me to watch the sun rise on this day. As I exited my home I could see the moon in its full brilliance was setting as well.

I stood on the shoreline and prayed for infinite knowledge. I knew the day was very special as I was aligned between both horizons standing on the edge of the gateway between our earth and heavenly planes.

I blessed Father Sun and Sister Moon, Father God and Mother Earth. The four corners of our existence - North, South, East and West. In that moment I celebrated the birth of a new day, the peace of the moon's set, the grace of a sunset and the life of a moonrise? The true cycle of life was in perfect synchronicity of time and space to receive words of Grace.

Our Earth classroom is filled with so many joys and challenges. Sometimes it is overwhelming to think about all the responsibilities you have. The financial burdens, the chores, the children, the job, the house, the car, the committees, the never ending list of importance is crammed into the 24 hours of a day. It is difficult to find time for peace and balance within your busy life. These graceful messages are to provide you with a momentary gift to lighten your heart to carry you forward. Each of these messages are to be read independently. Read one message then stop, and reflect upon the numerous undertones and meanings. Be joyful and blessed.

- Embrace the greatest gift of life. It is Love which is found within you.

- Absorb Truth though all aspects of your existence.

- Life is full of an Eternity of knowledge.

- Ageless and un-bounding strength comes from the power of the sea or the ability to move and change with the tides.

- The Solid foundation of Mother Earth is made of tiny grains of sand -- All as One.

- Dream with the clouds - ever-changing, gracefully floating and wisp along to be born.

- Be assured of the life cycle – day, night, or seasonal. All life is on the Wheel of Time.

- The Earth is made of elements – Fire, Water, Earth and Air. Take time to understand and honor each.

- Extremes can create elemental transformation which are not easily recovered.

- Water can be boiled or frozen to create melting/steam or ice each reformed under pressure into a new existence.

- Listen to knowledge with your heart. Feel the Divine guidance, to direct your destiny.

- Listen to the call of nature to truly connect.

- The Sun/Son provides a path of light to follow.

- Set your intention through meditation in the morning then move forward with your day.

- Reflect upon your lessons of the day before bed and be grateful.

- Waves provide the high points of your life.

- Run and play with abandon as a dog or child – eager, new, fresh - full of presence and joy each day.

- Rest in the arms of Love.

- Fly above the horizon, but low enough to see and experience life.

- Leave this earth with a graceful impression of your life's' existence.

- Don't always exert all your energy flapping your wings to fly, it is just as important to glide on the winds of the world.

- Small annoyances are as gnats. They can be easily ignored, shoed away or one can get caught up and overwhelmed by the tiniest of mites.

- Do you ever take time to remove your shoes to experience the world below your feet?

- Listen to the call of a bird. What are the words of its wisdom?

- Sand is made of many shapes, sizes and colors. Each grain of sand is unique. Yet together, the grains create a solid surface of One.

- Are you watching where you are going so closely that you forget to look up and celebrate where you are today?

- When the sun or moon sets, it never goes away, it just moves beyond your sight.

- The Sun is always present even above the storm clouds.

- Walking works out the kinks both within and without.

- Grass grows many tiny and strong roots but is made to bend and move as the winds blow.

- Fog is a light shroud covering what you truly know is already there.

- The earliest and latest part of daylight showcases the most brilliant colors of a day.

- Look below the surface to see an entirely different existence.

- When you walk as a pair, you hear one another, when you walk alone you listen within.

- Breathe in new life, Exhale the unwanted.

- Why do we hold on so tightly to what we no longer need or want?

- Walk with strength and courage, but look up to see where you are going.

- The light on earth can become so bright that you can't look at it. Focus on the reflection to get a true understanding.

- Sometimes it seems like you are going in circles, but isn't it important to see where you have been to know where to go.

- Rest in the knowledge of this single moment. Be totally present.

- Sometimes it seems like you are going in circles, but isn't it important to see where you have been to know where to go.

- Look for what is causing the ripples below.

- We run to beat the clock – but can you ever recapture the time that is gone doing so?

- A soft breeze is a welcome comfort and a harsh wind will close the door.

- What kind of impression are YOU leaving behind?

- A shadow can often tell the inside story.

- Welcome each day with fresh eyes and a grateful spirit.

- A difficult life full of challenges creates a hard shell, but when you look within it is still created from a soft soul.

- What lays below the surface is unknown. It isn't good or bad but has the opportunity to be discovered.

- The crack of dawn creates a cusp for your existence.

- Traveling to new destinations is just as exciting within as you travel without.

HOMEWORK:

Copy the messages onto paper, cut, fold and put into a container to draw one out on a regular basis. A blessings to carry you through your day.

EPILOGUE
A Special Note to You

The topics contained in this book are Divinely Inspired. With the highest of intent and purposeful practice, my ability to heal has growth beyond what my mind could imagine!

As my journey in faith and self-discovery continues, so will yours. That is what this book is really all about. Looking beyond and seeing what can be and then choosing to live that way.

As soon as I finished this book another has begun "Messages and Moments to Guide Your Light". So if you liked this book keep your eyes open and Spirit has a great future for us both.

This book has been an amazing journey for me and I hope for each of you. My wish is for many blessings to each of you, my dear friends. Thank you for joining this personal journey of self-development. May God's light shine brightly upon your life, in all that you do and in all that you are!

A very special thank you to all who helped make this dream a reality!

REFERENCE / RESOURCES

Hay House Inc. (2006). *Ask your Guides* by Sonia Choquette.
Hay House Inc. (2011). *The Angel Therapy* by Doreen Virtue.
Hay House Inc. (1998). *Chakra Clearing* by Doreen Virtue.
Whitaker House (2007). *The Gifts of the Spirit* by Derek Prince.
The Catholic Faith 4, no.2 (1998). *Guardian Angels* by Christine J. Murray.
Walking Stick Press (2003). *The Crystal Bible* by Judy Hall.
God the Great Spirit by Bonnie Moss.
Hay House Inc. (2005). *Angel Medicine* by Doreen Virtue.
Webster Dictionary, www.webster-dictionary.org.
Patty Wigington, www.pagan.wiccan.about.com.
N.S. Gill *Bible,* www.Wikipedia.org/wiki/Bible.
Listening, www.changingminds.org.
Meditations by Ashkhen Keshishian.

SUGGESTED READING LIST

Eckhart Teachings (1999). *The Power of Now* by Eckhart Tolle
Mind-Body Energy Therapy by Marlene Henkin. www.henkinenergytherapy.com.
Atria Books (2003). *The True Power of Water* by Dr. Masaru Emoto.
Hay House, Inc. (2006). *Animal Sport Guides* by Steven D. Farmer, Ph.D.